INTRODUCTION TO ARTIFICIAL INTELLIGENCE

INTRODUCTION TO ARTIFICIAL INTELLIGENCE

ERIC FRICK

Destin Learning

CONTENTS

CHAPTER 1

Introduction

This Introduction sets the stage for the exploration of Artificial Intelligence (AI) in this book, addressing readers' expectations and framing the content's scope and purpose.

Welcome to Introduction to Artificial Intelligence! (1.1)

This introductory section extends a warm welcome to readers, outlining the author's intention to demystify AI. It emphasizes making the subject approachable and digestible for a broad audience, ensuring the book's content is not only comprehensive but also concise for a reasonable reading length.

The Significance of AI in the Modern World (1.2)

This part highlights AI's transformative role in various industries and everyday life. It discusses how AI is revolutionizing healthcare, finance, manufacturing, and other sectors, and delves into its broader societal and economic impacts, showcasing AI as a pivotal technology in the modern era.

Target Audience and Approach of the Book (1.3)

The section identifies the book's target audience, which includes aspiring AI professionals, industry practitioners, academics, tech enthusiasts, and policymakers. The approach is tailored to be accessible, engaging, and comprehensive, with a focus on real-world applications and case studies to illuminate AI's practical and theoretical aspects.

Section 1.0 offers a welcoming introduction, setting the tone for a book that seeks to provide a clear and thorough understanding of AI. It establishes the significance of AI in various realms and outlines the book's approach to make AI relatable and understandable for a diverse range of readers.

1.1 Welcome to Introduction to Artificial Intelligence!

Welcome to the Book! Welcome to "Introduction to Artificial Intelligence"! I am thrilled to have you embark on this journey through the fascinating world of AI with me. This book is designed to be your guide into the often-intimidating realm of Artificial Intelligence.

Demystifying AI My primary goal in writing this book was to demystify AI. There's a lot of buzz around the term, but what does it really mean? How does it work? These are some of the questions I aim to answer in a clear and concise manner, stripping away the complexities to make AI approachable for everyone.

A Wide View of AI Artificial Intelligence is a large and diverse technical community with numerous subfields and specialties. This book aims to provide a wide view of AI, covering its various aspects. From machine learning to neural networks, from natural language processing to robotics, we will explore the many faces of AI and how they are impacting the world we live in.

Insights on Innovations and the Future of AI AI is not just about what's happening now; it's also about what the future holds. This book includes insights into recent innovations in AI, as well as educated predictions about where AI is headed. What are the next big breakthroughs? How will AI continue to evolve? These are some of the forward-looking topics we will delve into.

Ease of Reading and Understanding I understand that AI can seem complex and overwhelming. That's why I've made a conscious effort to ensure that this book is easy to read and understand, irrespective of your background in technology. The concepts are explained in simple terms, with real-world examples and analogies to make them relatable.

A Book of Reasonable Length Time is precious, and I respect that. Therefore, I've ensured that this book is of a reasonable length - comprehensive enough to cover the essential aspects of AI but concise enough that you can finish it in a reasonable amount of time. Whether you're a busy professional, a student, or someone with a casual interest in AI, you'll find this book to be an efficient and enjoyable read.

Thank You for Your Purchase! Thank you sincerely for choosing this book. I'm delighted you are here and hope that this journey through the realms of AI enlightens, educates, and inspires you. Let's begin this exciting exploration of one of the most revolutionary technologies of our time!

1.2 The Significance of AI in the Modern World

The advent of Artificial Intelligence (AI) has brought about a paradigm shift in the modern world, redefining how we interact with technology and each other. AI's influence spans various sectors, driving innovation, efficiency, and solving complex problems that were once thought insurmountable. This section explores the multifaceted significance of AI in today's world, underscoring its impact on different aspects of society, economy, and daily life.

Revolutionizing Industries

AI's transformative impact spans several key industries:

In healthcare, AI is revolutionizing the field by offering more accurate diagnostics and personalized treatment plans. Technologies such as predictive analytics and medical imaging analysis are leading to significant improvements in patient outcomes. This encompasses everything from early disease detection to customized therapy approaches, greatly enhancing healthcare delivery and efficiency.

In finance, AI is reshaping operations through its capabilities in fraud detection, algorithmic trading, and personalization of banking services. These advancements are crucial in heightening security measures and enriching customer experiences, as AI can analyze vast amounts of financial data to identify irregular patterns, optimize investment strategies, and tailor services to individual client needs.

Manufacturing is also witnessing a paradigm shift due to AI. With AI-driven automation and predictive maintenance, the sector is experiencing heightened productivity and reduced operational costs. AI systems in manufacturing can predict machinery maintenance needs, optimize production lines, and manage supply chains more efficiently, leading to a substantial increase in overall efficiency and reduction in production downtimes.

These examples highlight AI's role as a major catalyst for innovation and efficiency across diverse sectors, signifying its growing importance in the modern industrial landscape.

Enhancing Everyday Life

AI is significantly enhancing everyday life in various ways:

AI-powered smart home devices, such as voice assistants, are revolutionizing home management, offering convenience and elevating the quality of life. They automate household tasks, provide security, and facilitate seamless control of home environments.

In retail and entertainment, AI's capacity to process vast data sets enables highly personalized experiences. This includes tailored shopping recommendations and content curation, which cater to individual preferences and enhance user engagement. AI analyzes user behavior and preferences to deliver these customized experiences, making everyday activities more aligned with personal tastes and needs.

Driving Technological Innovation

AI's role in technological innovation is profound and wide-ranging:

In computing, AI has been a crucial driver in advancing fields such as quantum computing. It has significantly enhanced computational capabilities, enabling the processing of complex, large-scale problems far beyond the scope of traditional computing methods.

In the realm of research and development, AI accelerates the pace of discovery across various scientific disciplines. It contributes to groundbreaking advancements in areas like environmental science, where it aids in climate modeling and ecosystem analysis, and in space exploration, assisting in data analysis from space missions and development of autonomous systems for exploration. This acceleration is reshaping the landscape of scientific research, opening new frontiers for exploration and understanding.

Societal Impact

AI's societal impact is profound and diverse, particularly in education and environmental solutions:

In education, AI is transforming the landscape by offering personalized learning experiences and automating administrative tasks. This not only makes education more accessible and tailored to individual needs but also streamlines educational processes, allowing educators to focus more on teaching and less on administrative duties.

In the realm of environmental solutions, AI plays a crucial role in monitoring and understanding environmental changes. It aids in developing effective strategies for sustainability and combating climate change, analyzing vast amounts of environmental data to inform decision-making and policy development. This application of AI is essential.

AI's societal impact extends into the healthcare sector as well. AI is revolutionizing healthcare by improving diagnostic accuracy, enhancing treatment personalization, and streamlining administrative processes. This technology enables more efficient patient care and management, contributing to better health outcomes and more effective healthcare systems. The implementation of AI in healthcare demonstrates its potential to profoundly improve the quality and accessibility of medical services.

Economic Implications

The economic implications of AI are far-reaching, particularly in terms of job creation and market transformation. While AI and automation might lead to the displacement of certain jobs, they also pave the way for new types of employment and necessitate the development of new skill sets. This shift in the job market reflects the evolving nature of work in an AI-driven economy, highlighting the need for workers to adapt and acquire new competencies to thrive in this changing landscape.

AI's influence on the global economy is substantial. It acts as a catalyst for growth, innovation, and competitiveness, reshaping industries and economies worldwide. AI's capability to enhance productivity, foster new market opportunities, and drive technological advancement positions it as a pivotal element in the global economic landscape. This influence is evident across sectors, from healthcare and finance to manufacturing and technology, underscoring AI's role in shaping economic trends and futures.

Ethical and Policy Considerations

The integration of AI into various aspects of life raises significant ethical and policy considerations. Privacy and security concerns are paramount as AI systems often handle sensitive data, necessitating robust measures to protect this information. Moreover, the development and application of AI require clear ethical guidelines and regulatory frameworks to ensure responsible use and prevent misuse. These considerations are crucial for maintaining trust in AI technologies and ensuring they are used in a way that benefits society as a whole.

Summary

The significance of AI in the modern world is profound and far-reaching. It has not only revolutionized industries and enhanced daily life but also driven technological innovation and had a substantial societal and economic impact. As AI continues to evolve, it presents both opportunities and challenges, necessitating careful consideration of ethical, privacy, and policy issues. The future trajectory of AI will significantly influence the direction of human progress and societal transformation.

1.3 Target Audience and Approach of the Book

In crafting a book on Artificial Intelligence (AI), it's essential to define the target audience and the approach to effectively communicate the complexities and nuances of AI. This section outlines the intended readership of the book and the methodological approach adopted to make the subject matter accessible and engaging to that audience.

Identifying the Target Audience

Aspiring AI Professionals: Individuals looking to enter the field of AI, including students, early-career professionals, and those transitioning from other industries.

Industry Practitioners: Professionals in sectors like healthcare, finance, and technology who seek to understand how AI can be applied in their domains.

Academics and Researchers: Those in academic and research roles who require a deeper understanding of AI's current state and future potential.

General Tech Enthusiasts: Individuals with a keen interest in technology and AI, looking to stay informed about the latest developments and trends.

Policy Makers and Ethicists: Individuals involved in creating policies or ethical guidelines for AI, needing a comprehensive understanding of the technology and its societal impact.

Approach of the Book

Balancing Technicality with Accessibility: While covering essential technical aspects, the book is written in an accessible language to cater to readers with varying levels of AI knowledge.

Use of Case Studies and Real-World Examples: Incorporating case studies to demonstrate AI's practical applications, making the content relatable and easier to comprehend.

Comprehensive Coverage: Providing a broad overview of AI, including its history, current technologies, applications, ethical considerations, and future prospects.

Interactive and Engaging Content: Utilizing visual aids, interactive examples, and thought-provoking exercises to engage the reader actively.

Resource Inclusion: Offering additional resources such as references, websites, and further reading materials for readers who wish to delve deeper into specific topics.

Summary

The book "Introduction to Artificial Intelligence" is tailored for a diverse readership, ranging from aspiring AI professionals to industry practitioners, academics, tech enthusiasts, and policy makers. It adopts a balanced approach, combining technical depth with accessibility, and enriches its narrative with real-world examples, case studies, and interactive content. The goal is to provide a comprehensive yet understandable overview of AI, catering to the varied needs and interests of the readers, and encouraging them to further explore the dynamic and ever-evolving field of AI.

CHAPTER 2

History of Artificial Intelligence

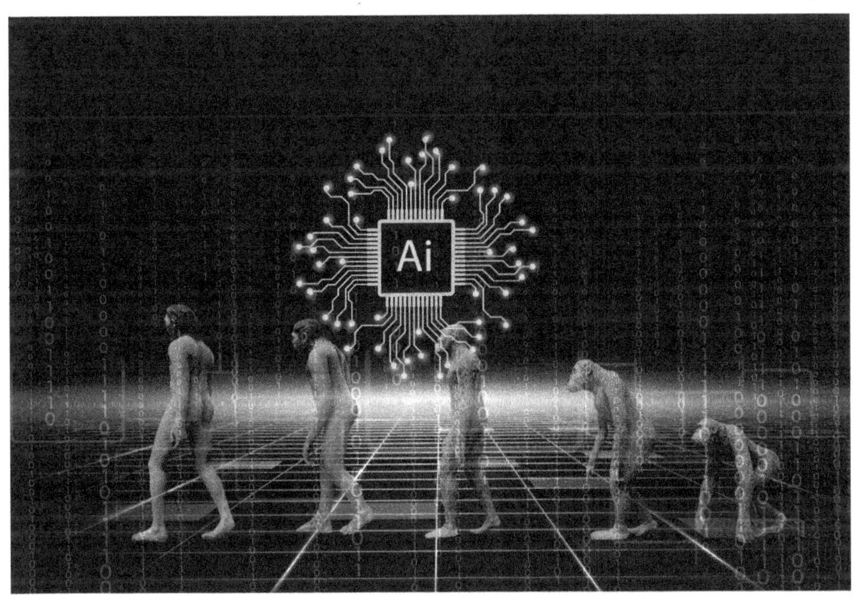

The History of Artificial Intelligence provides a comprehensive overview of the evolution of AI, tracing its roots from philosophical concepts to its current status as a pivotal technology in the modern world.

Early Concepts and Philosophical Roots (2.1)

This subsection explores the philosophical and theoretical foundations of AI. It begins with the ancient philosophers' contemplations about intelligence and consciousness, moving through the Renaissance period's fascination with automata, and into the significant contributions of 17th and 19th-century thinkers like René Descartes and George Boole. This historical backdrop sets the stage for understanding AI's evolution, highlighting the longstanding human intrigue with replicating intelligence.

Milestones in AI Development (2.2)

This part outlines the key historical milestones in the field of AI. Starting with the Turing Test proposed by Alan Turing in the 1950s, it covers the inception of the term "Artificial Intelligence" at the 1956 Dartmouth Conference, the development of expert systems in the 1960s, the AI Winter periods, and the eventual shift towards machine learning. Significant breakthroughs, such as IBM's Deep Blue chess program and the rise of deep learning, are discussed, showcasing the major achievements and challenges in AI development.

Evolution of AI: From Symbolic AI to Machine Learning (2.3)

This subsection details the transition from early AI based on symbolic logic (also known as "Good Old-Fashioned AI") to the contemporary era of machine learning and neural networks. It examines the limitations of Symbolic AI in handling complex, real-world data, leading to the emergence of machine learning approaches that focus on data-driven decision-making and pattern recognition. The impact of neural networks and deep learning in advancing AI capabilities is highlighted, emphasizing the shift towards more adaptive and sophisticated AI systems.

Section 2.0 The History of Artificial Intelligence provides a thorough examination of AI's origins, developmental milestones, and its transformative journey. From philosophical speculations and early innovations to breakthroughs in computing and algorithmic development, this section underscores the diverse and evolving nature of AI, marking its transition from a theoretical concept to a transformative technology that continues to shape the future.

2.1 Early Concepts and Philosophical Roots

The journey of artificial intelligence (AI) begins not in the realm of computer science, but within the ancient tapestries of philosophy and early innovations. This section explores the philosophical roots and early concepts that laid the foundation for modern AI.

The Dawn of AI Thought in Philosophy

The conceptual roots of Artificial Intelligence (AI) in philosophy stretch back to ancient times and evolve through significant historical periods, influencing the development of modern AI.

Ancient Philosophers and Automata

The fascination with endowing inanimate objects with intelligence has its origins in ancient Greece. Philosophers like Aristotle and Plato explored the nature of thought, consciousness, and the possibility of creating mechanical minds. Aristotle, in particular, pondered the nature of automata and the principles of causation and movement, which can be seen as early steps toward understanding automated processes.

The idea of automata, self-moving devices, was also reflected in myths and legends of ancient civilizations, indicating a longstanding human intrigue with creating life-like, intelligent machines.

Renaissance Automata and Mechanical Thought

During the Renaissance, a renewed interest in science and invention led to the creation of intricate automata. Inventors and thinkers like Leonardo da Vinci designed mechanical devices that could mimic the movements of humans and animals. Da Vinci's sketches and designs, including his famous robotic knight, showcased an early fascination with mechanical intelligence and the potential of machines.

This era represented a significant shift in thinking about the capabilities of machines and the potential for automata to replicate aspects of human intelligence and behavior.

Descartes and Dualism René Descartes, a prominent 17th-century philosopher, introduced the concept of mind-body dualism, which became a critical philosophical foundation in understanding consciousness and intelligence. His theory posited a distinction between the physical body and the non-physical mind, raising questions about the nature of thought and self-awareness.

Descartes' famous statement "Cogito, ergo sum" (I think, therefore I am) emphasized the centrality of thought and cognition as the essence of existence and identity. This perspective laid the groundwork for later philosophical and scientific inquiries into the nature of intelligence, both human and artificial.

Logical Foundations and Theoretical Constructs

The development of Artificial Intelligence (AI) is deeply rooted in logical and mathematical theories that laid the groundwork for modern computing and AI concepts.

Boolean Logic and Mathematical Foundations

George Boole, a 19th-century mathematician, made a pivotal contribution to the foundations of computer science and AI with the development of Boolean algebra. Boolean algebra presents a logical framework for working with binary variables and operations, which are true or false (or equivalently, 1 or 0). This system of logic became fundamental in the design and functioning of digital circuits and computers. Boolean algebra allows for the representation and manipulation of logical statements and is used in the creation of algorithms and computational processes. Boole's work provided a mathematical means to model and solve logical problems, laying the foundation for logical reasoning processes in computers.

Alan Turing and the Concept of Computation

Alan Turing, a 20th-century mathematician and computer scientist, significantly advanced the understanding of computation and its possibilities. He introduced the concept of the Turing machine, an abstract computational model that is capable of simulating any algorithm's logic.

The Turing machine is a theoretical construct that helped define the capabilities and limits of what can be computed. Turing's work, including his conceptualization of algorithmic processing and the Turing Test for machine intelligence, laid the intellectual foundation for modern computing and the concept of AI. Turing's ideas not only shaped the development of early computers but also framed the ongoing discussions about the nature and potential of artificial intelligence. His contributions are considered fundamental to the field and continue to influence AI research and development.

Early Speculations on Artificial Intelligence

The concept of Artificial Intelligence (AI) has been the subject of speculation and imagination long before it became a scientific reality. This early speculation played a crucial role in shaping the development and public perception of AI.

Science Fiction and Visionary Writers

Science fiction writers like Isaac Asimov and Arthur C. Clarke were instrumental in painting vivid pictures of a future where intelligent machines played a central role. Their stories and novels explored the possibilities, challenges, and ethical dilemmas associated with AI.

Isaac Asimov, in particular, is renowned for his "Three Laws of Robotics," a set of ethical guidelines for intelligent machines that have become a staple in AI discourse. Asimov's stories often revolved around the interactions between humans and robots, exploring the complexities of such relationships.

Arthur C. Clarke's works, including "2001: A Space Odyssey," imagined advanced AI systems with profound implications for humanity. His depiction of AI ranged from benevolent to existential threats, reflecting the diverse potential outcomes of AI development.

Early Philosophical Debates

In the mid-20th century, philosophical debates about AI began to take shape, with thinkers like John Searle and Herbert Simon contributing to the discourse. These debates revolved around the nature of intelligence and consciousness and the possibility of replicating these traits in machines. John Searle's "Chinese Room" argument questioned the ability of computers to truly "understand" or possess consciousness, even if they could simulate human-like responses. This argument sparked discussions about the nature of understanding and the limits of artificial minds.

Herbert Simon, a polymath and one of the pioneers in AI research, held a more optimistic view of AI's potential. He was instrumental in developing early AI programs and theories, contributing to the understanding of problem-solving and decision-making processes in machines.

These early philosophical debates set the stage for ongoing ethical and philosophical discussions in AI, addressing questions about the nature of intelligence, the potential of machines to replicate human cognition, and the ethical implications of such advancements.

Summary

The philosophical roots of AI are deep and diverse, spanning from ancient Greek thought to 20th-century logical theories. These early concepts provide a crucial context for understanding how AI evolved.

Philosophical debates on consciousness, intelligence, and mechanical minds paved the way for the development of modern AI. The transition from speculative thought to tangible technological advancement marks a significant shift in human capability and understanding. This rich history underscores the importance of multidisciplinary perspectives in the evolution of AI, bridging the gap between philosophical inquiry and technological innovation.

2.2 Milestones in AI Development

The development of Artificial Intelligence (AI) has been marked by several key milestones that have significantly advanced the field. This section outlines these pivotal moments, tracing the evolution of AI from its theoretical origins to its current state.

The Birth of AI as a Discipline

The formal inception of Artificial Intelligence (AI) as a scientific discipline occurred in the mid-20th century, marked by two significant events that laid the foundation for the field's development.

1950s – The Turing Test Proposed by Alan Turing in a 1950 paper titled "Computing Machinery and Intelligence," the Turing Test became a seminal concept in AI. Turing proposed a test to determine a machine's ability to exhibit intelligent behavior indistinguishable from that of a human. In the Turing Test, a human evaluator interacts with an unseen interlocutor, which could be either a human or a machine, and attempts to determine which it is based solely on the responses. If the machine is able to convince the evaluator that it is human, it is said to have passed the test.

The Turing Test set an early benchmark for machine intelligence and sparked debates about the nature of intelligence and the potential for machines to replicate human cognitive abilities. It remains a touchstone in discussions about AI, even as the field has evolved beyond Turing's initial vision.

1956 – Dartmouth Conference The Dartmouth Conference, held in 1956 at Dartmouth College, is widely considered the official birth of AI as a scientific discipline. Organized by John McCarthy, Marvin Minsky, Nathaniel Rochester, and Claude Shannon, the conference brought together leading scientists and mathematicians to discuss the potential of machines to simulate aspects of human intelligence.

It was at this conference that John McCarthy coined the term "Artificial Intelligence," defining it as the science and engineering of making intelligent machines. The conference participants outlined the initial goals of AI research, including the development of machines that could use language, form abstractions and concepts, solve problems reserved for humans, and improve themselves.

The Dartmouth Conference set the stage for AI research in the decades that followed, establishing AI as a distinct field of study and inspiring a generation of researchers to explore the possibilities of intelligent machines.

Early Successes and Theoretical Advances

The development of AI in the 1960s and 1970s saw significant milestones and theoretical breakthroughs that played a crucial role in shaping the field.

1960s – Expert Systems

The 1960s marked the emergence of expert systems, one of the earliest successful applications of AI. Expert systems were designed to emulate the decision-making abilities of human experts in specific domains, such as medicine, engineering, or finance. One of the first and most notable expert systems was DENDRAL, developed at Stanford University in the mid-1960s. DENDRAL was a pioneering program in the field of chemical informatics, designed to analyze chemical mass spectrometry data and infer the possible molecular structures of organic compounds.

These systems utilized a rule-based approach, where knowledge and rules about a particular domain were encoded into the system. By applying these rules to new data, expert systems could make recommendations or decisions, simulating the reasoning process of human experts.

1970s – Backpropagation in Neural Networks

In 1974, Paul Werbos conceptualized the backpropagation algorithm, a fundamental mechanism for training neural networks. Backpropagation is a method used to calculate the gradient of a loss function with respect to the weights of the network, allowing for efficient optimization during training.

Although Werbos' work laid the foundation for training multi-layer neural networks, the significance of backpropagation was not fully recognized until the 1980s. It was then that researchers began to appreciate its power in enabling neural networks to learn complex patterns and relationships in data.

The development of backpropagation represented a major theoretical advance in AI and contributed to the resurgence of neural networks in the 1980s, ultimately leading to the modern era of deep learning.

AI Winter and the Shift in Focus

The development of AI has not been a steady ascent; it has experienced periods of both heightened enthusiasm and significant setbacks. One such period, known as the "AI Winter," occurred in the 1980s and led to a pivotal shift in the field.

1980s – The First AI Winter

The early 1980s witnessed a downturn in the AI field, commonly referred to as the "AI Winter." This period was characterized by reduced funding, waning interest, and a general skepticism about the potential of AI. The AI Winter was largely a result of inflated expectations from earlier decades that did not materialize, coupled with technical limitations of the time. The challenges faced by AI during this period included the limitations of rule-based expert systems, which struggled with handling complex or ambiguous data, and the inability of early neural networks to scale effectively.

The reduced funding and interest during the AI Winter led to a reevaluation of approaches in AI research and a dampening of the over-optimistic predictions that had previously characterized the field.

Late 1980s – Rise of Machine Learning*

Towards the late 1980s, a significant shift occurred in AI, with a growing focus on probabilistic and statistical methods. This shift was marked by the development and adoption of machine learning algorithms, which offered a new paradigm for building AI systems. Notable developments during this period included the advancement of decision tree algorithms, which provided a simple yet effective method for classification and regression tasks, and the exploration of reinforcement learning, where agents learn to make decisions by interacting with their environment.

The rise of machine learning rejuvenated the AI field, laying the groundwork for more robust and adaptable AI systems. This shift represented a move away from hard-coded knowledge and rules towards models that could learn from data and improve their performance over time.

The Resurgence of Neural Networks and Deep Learning

The late 1990s and early 2000s marked a significant turning point in AI with the resurgence of neural networks and the emergence of deep learning, leading to groundbreaking advancements in the field.

1997 – Deep Blue Defeats Kasparov

In 1997, a major milestone in AI was achieved when IBM's Deep Blue, a computer chess program, defeated Garry Kasparov, the reigning world chess champion, in a highly publicized match. This event was significant as it showcased the advanced strategic capabilities of AI systems.

Deep Blue's victory was a result of a combination of brute-force computing power and sophisticated algorithms for evaluating and selecting chess moves. The system was capable of evaluating millions of positions per second, using a combination of advanced search algorithms and domain-specific heuristics. The success of Deep Blue demonstrated the potential of AI in complex problem-solving and strategic thinking, sparking renewed interest and investment in AI research.

2006 – The Term 'Deep Learning' Coined

A pivotal moment in the resurgence of neural networks occurred in 2006 when Geoffrey Hinton and his colleagues introduced the concept of 'deep learning.' The term 'deep learning' was coined to emphasize the use of multiple layers in neural networks, which allowed for the modeling of complex patterns and relationships in data.

Hinton and his team demonstrated that deep neural networks, when trained with sufficient data and computational power, could achieve remarkable performance in tasks such as image and speech recognition. This was a departure from earlier neural networks, which were typically shallow and limited in their capabilities. The introduction of deep learning led to a series of groundbreaking advancements in AI, including significant improvements in computer vision, natural language processing, and other areas that had previously been challenging for traditional machine learning methods. Deep learning has since become a cornerstone of modern AI, driving the development of highly capable AI systems and applications across various industries and domains.

Recent Breakthroughs and Mainstream Integration

The 2010s marked a period of significant advancements in AI, with breakthroughs in key areas like natural language processing (NLP) and computer vision, as well as the integration of AI into various aspects of everyday life.

2010s – Advancements in NLP and Computer Vision

The 2010s witnessed remarkable progress in NLP and computer vision, two areas where deep learning has had a profound impact. These advancements have been demonstrated through technologies such as Google's BERT (Bidirectional Encoder Representations from Transformers) in NLP and significant strides in image recognition algorithms.

In NLP, models like BERT achieved new levels of performance in understanding and generating human language, greatly improving the capabilities of machines in tasks such as language translation, text summarization, and question-answering. These models leverage deep learning to process and interpret language with a level of sophistication that was previously unattainable.

In computer vision, advancements in deep learning led to more accurate and efficient image recognition systems. These systems are capable of identifying and classifying objects in images and videos with high precision, enabling applications ranging from facial recognition to medical image analysis.

2010s Onwards – AI in Everyday Life

The integration of AI into everyday life became increasingly prominent during the 2010s. Virtual assistants like Apple's Siri, Amazon's Alexa, and Google Assistant brought AI into homes, providing users with voice-activated assistance for a range of tasks and queries.

Advancements in autonomous vehicles represent another significant area where AI has made inroads into daily life. Developments in self-driving car technology, powered by AI algorithms for perception, decision-making, and navigation, showcased the potential for AI to transform transportation.

AI's integration extends beyond these examples, impacting sectors such as healthcare, finance, retail, and entertainment. AI-driven applications and services have become more common, demonstrating the practical utility and societal impact of AI in various forms.

Summary

In summary, the journey of Artificial Intelligence (AI) is characterized by a series of groundbreaking advancements, periods of skepticism, and remarkable achievements. From its inception in the mid-20th century, AI has evolved significantly, with key developments in areas like deep learning and natural language processing (NLP). Initially rooted in academic and theoretical concepts, AI has transcended its origins to become an integral part of the modern world, influencing various industries and aspects of daily life.

The milestones in AI's history reflect an evolving understanding of its potential and capabilities. This evolution underscores the dynamic and ever-progressing nature of AI as a field. As AI continues to advance, it consistently pushes the boundaries of what machines are capable of, demonstrating its transformative impact on technology and society.

2.3 Evolution of AI: From Symbolic AI to Machine Learning

This section "Evolution of AI: From Symbolic AI to Machine Learning (2.3)" details the paradigm shift in artificial intelligence (AI) from initial models based on symbolic logic to contemporary approaches centered around machine learning and neural networks. It delves into the challenges faced by early Symbolic AI systems, particularly their struggles with processing and interpreting complex, real-world data.

The emergence of machine learning is then examined, noting its emphasis on learning from data, making decisions, and recognizing patterns without explicit programming. The section also underscores the significant role of neural networks and deep learning, which have been instrumental in propelling AI forward, leading to more adaptive and sophisticated systems capable of tasks like image and speech recognition. This transition marks a critical evolution in AI, showcasing the move from rule-based systems to those that learn and improve autonomously.

The Era of Symbolic AI

The era of Symbolic AI, also known as "Good Old-Fashioned AI" (GOFAI), represents a significant phase in the development of Artificial Intelligence, with its roots deeply embedded in symbolic logic and its application in expert systems and logic programming.

Origins in Symbolic Logic

Symbolic AI emerged from the foundational work in symbolic logic by pioneering figures like Alan Turing and John McCarthy. This approach to AI was based on the notion that human thought and problem-solving could be represented through symbols and logical operations.

The underlying principle of Symbolic AI was that all knowledge and reasoning could be represented using symbols and that logical rules could be applied to these symbols to perform reasoning and problem-solving tasks. This approach sought to replicate human cognitive processes by manipulating symbols that represented concepts and relationships.

Alan Turing's work on formalizing the concepts of computation and algorithmic processes provided a theoretical foundation for Symbolic AI. John McCarthy, often credited with coining the term "Artificial Intelligence," further advanced this approach with his work on formalizing logic-based AI and the development of the Lisp programming language, which became a staple in AI research.

Expert Systems and Logic Programming

During the 1960s and 70s, AI research was heavily focused on the development of expert systems. These systems represented a practical application of Symbolic AI, aiming to emulate human expertise in specific domains such as medical diagnosis, geological exploration, and legal reasoning.

Expert systems were built using predefined rules and logic that encapsulated the knowledge of human experts in a particular field. By applying these rules to new situations, the systems could make inferences and decisions, mimicking the decision-making process of human experts.

These systems were among the first AI applications to be used in commercial and industrial settings, demonstrating the potential of AI to solve complex problems and provide expert-level advice in specialized areas.

Limitations of Symbolic AI and the Shift Towards Learning

While Symbolic AI, or "Good Old-Fashioned AI" (GOFAI), laid the groundwork for early AI development, it eventually encountered significant limitations, particularly in its ability to handle real-world complexity. This led to a shift in focus towards the development of learning algorithms.

Inflexibility and Brittleness

One of the main limitations of Symbolic AI was its inflexibility and brittleness when faced with real-world scenarios. Symbolic AI systems operated based on a set of predefined rules and knowledge explicitly encoded by humans. While effective in controlled or well-defined environments, these systems struggled to adapt to new, unforeseen, or ambiguous situations.

The rule-based nature of Symbolic AI meant that it lacked the ability to generalize beyond the specific scenarios for which it was programmed. When encountering data or situations that did not fit within the predefined rules, these systems often failed to perform adequately. This limitation was particularly evident in domains where the complexity and variability of real-world data were high, such as natural language understanding and visual perception.

The Need for Learning Algorithms

Recognizing the limitations of purely rule-based systems, researchers in the AI field began to explore learning algorithms as an alternative approach. The aim was to develop systems that could learn from data, adapt to new information, and make decisions based on learned patterns and relationships, rather than solely relying on predefined rules.

This shift towards learning algorithms marked a transition from a top-down approach, where knowledge is hand-coded into systems, to a bottom-up approach, where systems derive knowledge from data. Machine learning, and later deep learning, emerged as key methodologies in this new paradigm, enabling AI systems to automatically learn and improve from experience.

The development of learning algorithms represented a significant advancement in AI, allowing for greater flexibility, adaptability, and robustness in AI systems. This shift laid the foundation for many of the modern AI applications we see today, from sophisticated natural language processing systems to advanced computer vision technologies.

The Rise of Machine Learning

The late 1980s and early 1990s marked a significant shift in the field of AI, with the emergence of machine learning, particularly statistical learning and neural networks, as dominant methodologies.

Statistical Learning and Data-Driven Approaches By the late 1980s and into the 1990s, the focus of AI research began to shift towards statistical methods and data-driven approaches, largely under the umbrella of machine learning. This transition was driven by several factors, including the increasing availability of large datasets and advancements in computational power.

Statistical learning approaches emphasized the use of data to train algorithms, enabling AI systems to develop models that could make predictions or decisions based on empirical evidence. This represented a move away from the rule-based systems of Symbolic AI, offering a more flexible and robust approach to dealing with real-world variability and complexity.

The rise of machine learning led to significant advancements in areas such as pattern recognition, natural language processing, and predictive analytics. Algorithms like decision trees, support vector machines, and Bayesian networks became popular tools for solving a wide range of AI problems.

The Development of Neural Networks

Parallel to the rise of statistical learning was the resurgence and development of neural networks. Neural networks are computational models inspired by the structure and function of biological neural networks in the brain. These systems learn to perform tasks by being exposed to numerous examples, generally without the need for task-specific programming.

The concept of neural networks had been around since the 1950s, but it wasn't until the 1980s and 1990s that significant advancements were made, particularly with the popularization of the backpropagation algorithm for training multi-layer networks. Neural networks became a powerful tool for AI, particularly in tasks involving pattern recognition, such as image and speech recognition. The flexibility and learning capabilities of neural networks made them suitable for a wide range of applications, setting the stage for the later development of deep learning.

The Breakthrough of Deep Learning

The advent of deep learning in the 2000s represented a significant milestone in the evolution of AI, particularly in the advancement of neural networks and their application to various complex tasks.

Advancements in Neural Networks

Deep learning, a subset of machine learning, involves the use of neural networks with multiple layers (hence "deep") that enable the learning of complex and hierarchical representations of data. This development was a significant leap forward from earlier neural networks, which typically had fewer layers and were limited in their capacity to process complex patterns.

The key to deep learning's success lies in its ability to automatically learn rich and abstract representations of data, which makes it highly effective for tasks involving large amounts of unstructured data, such as images, audio, and text.

Several factors contributed to the breakthrough of deep learning, including the availability of large datasets (big data), increased computational power (especially through the use of GPUs), and advancements in neural network architectures and training techniques.

Major Achievements of Deep Learning

Deep learning has led to remarkable achievements across various domains of AI:

- Mastering Complex Games: One of the most publicized achievements of deep learning was the development of systems like DeepMind's AlphaGo, which defeated world champion Go players. This accomplishment demonstrated the ability of deep learning systems to master complex strategies and decision-making in environments with vast possibilities.
- Improvements in Speech and Image Recognition: Deep learning has significantly advanced the fields of speech and image recognition. Convolutional Neural Networks (CNNs), a type of deep neural network, have become the standard in image recognition tasks, greatly enhancing the accuracy and efficiency of recognizing and classifying images. Similarly, deep learning has improved the accuracy of speech recognition systems, making technologies like voice assistants more reliable and widespread.
- Advancements in Natural Language Processing (NLP): Deep learning has revolutionized NLP, enabling more sophisticated understanding and generation of human language. This has led to advancements in machine translation, text generation, and sentiment analysis, among other applications.

AI in the Modern Era

Artificial Intelligence (AI) has become a pervasive and integral part of both everyday life and various industries in the modern era, driven largely by advancements in machine learning. As the field continues to evolve, it also faces new challenges and areas for continued development.

Integration into Everyday Life

Today, AI and machine learning have found applications in numerous aspects of daily life and industry, significantly impacting how businesses operate and how individuals interact with technology. In e-commerce, AI-driven recommendation systems personalize shopping experiences by analyzing consumer behavior and preferences, suggesting products that users are likely to purchase. These systems have become a staple in online retail platforms, enhancing customer engagement and sales.

In manufacturing, AI is used for predictive maintenance, where machine learning algorithms analyze data from equipment sensors to predict potential failures before they occur. This application of AI increases efficiency, reduces downtime, and saves costs by preemptively addressing maintenance issues.

Other examples of AI integration include virtual personal assistants (like Siri and Alexa), AI in healthcare for diagnostics and personalized treatment, autonomous vehicles, smart home devices, and more. These applications illustrate the widespread adoption and versatility of AI in enhancing various facets of modern life and business operations.

Continued Evolution and Challenges

As AI continues to evolve, the field faces several challenges that need to be addressed to ensure responsible and effective deployment of AI technologies:

- Ensuring Fairness: One of the key challenges is to ensure that AI systems are fair and do not perpetuate biases present in training data. This involves developing methods to detect and mitigate bias in AI algorithms to prevent unfair treatment or discrimination.
- Understanding AI Decision-Making (Explainability): As AI systems become more complex, particularly with the advent of

deep learning, understanding how these systems make decisions (known as explainability) is crucial. There is a growing need for AI to be transparent and interpretable, especially in critical applications like healthcare and criminal justice, where decisions have significant consequences.

- Other Challenges: Additional challenges include ensuring the privacy and security of data used in AI systems, addressing ethical concerns, managing the impact of AI on the workforce and employment, and developing robust and reliable AI systems that can operate safely in dynamic real-world environments.

Summary

In summary, he evolution of Artificial Intelligence (AI) from Symbolic AI to Machine Learning represents a significant shift in how AI systems approach problem-solving. Initially, early AI systems relied on hard-coded knowledge and logical inference, which proved limited in handling complex, real-world scenarios. The transition to machine learning, particularly with the advent of neural networks and deep learning, marked a profound expansion in AI's capabilities and applications.

This shift allowed AI systems to learn from data, adapt, and improve over time, demonstrating the adaptability and progressive nature of AI research. As a result, AI continues to advance towards more sophisticated and capable systems. The focus in AI research is increasingly on refining technologies, ensuring their ethical application, and exploring their potential in various domains. This continual advancement underscores the dynamic and evolving nature of AI.

2.4 Quiz - The History of Artificial Intelligence

Q1: Who proposed the Turing Test, a benchmark for determining a machine's capability to exhibit intelligent behavior?

1. Alan Turing
2. John McCarthy
3. Marvin Minsky
4. Isaac Newton

Q2: At which event was the term "Artificial Intelligence" first coined?

1. The Dartmouth Conference (1956)
2. The Turing Conference (1950)
3. The MIT AI Conference (1960)
4. The Stanford Symposium (1955)
   Correct Answer: a) The Dartmouth Conference (1956)

Q3: Which of the following is considered an early form of AI in history?

1. Calculators
2. Mechanical Clocks
3. Renaissance Automata
4. Telegraph Machines
   Correct Answer: c) Renaissance Automata

Q4: What was a significant achievement in AI during the 1990s?

1. The creation of the World Wide Web
2. The development of the first chatbot
3. IBM's Deep Blue defeating chess champion Garry Kasparov
4. The launch of the first smartphone

Q5: hat does Symbolic AI focus on?

1. Neural networks
2. Rule-based systems and logical reasoning
3. Data mining
4. Quantum computing

Q6: Who developed the concept of Boolean Logic, which is foundational in AI?

1. Alan Turing
2. John von Neumann
3. George Boole
4. Ada Lovelace

Q7: What marked the beginning of the 'AI Winter' in the 1980s?

1. Lack of interest in AI
2. Reduction in AI research funding
3. Overhyped AI expectations
4. Technical limitations in computing power

Q8: Which development signified a major shift in AI from rule-based systems to learning algorithms?

1. The introduction of expert systems
2. The rise of machine learning
3. The development of the first neural network
4. The invention of the microprocessor

Q9: What is the primary focus of 'Deep Learning' within AI?

1. Data privacy
2. Logical reasoning
3. Neural networks with many layers
4. Symbolic language processing

Q10: Which of the following was an early expert system used in AI?

1. ELIZA
2. DENDRAL
3. Watson
4. Siri
5.

CHAPTER 3

Fundamentals of Artificial Intelligence

Fundamentals of Artificial Intelligence provides an in-depth exploration of the core concepts and elements that constitute AI, offering insights into its nature, functionality, and the technologies underpinning it.

Understanding Intelligence: Human vs. Artificial (3.1)

This subsection delves into the comparative analysis of human and artificial intelligence. It discusses the characteristics of human intelligence, including reasoning, learning, and emotional depth, and contrasts these with the capabilities of AI. The focus is on highlighting the differences and similarities in how humans and AI systems process information, learn, and adapt.

Key Concepts in AI: Algorithms, Data, and Learning (3.2)

Here, the fundamental components driving AI systems are discussed. The section emphasizes the crucial role of algorithms in decision-making processes, the importance of data as the fuel for AI, and the concept of machine learning as the mechanism through which AI evolves and improves. It provides a comprehensive understanding of how these components interact to enable AI functionalities.

Overview of Machine Learning, Deep Learning, and Neural Networks (3.3)

This part offers a detailed overview of machine learning, deep learning, and neural networks, which are critical components of modern AI. It explains the basics of machine learning, its types (such as supervised, unsupervised, and reinforcement learning), and progresses to deep learning and neural networks, illustrating how these advanced techniques enable AI to perform complex tasks and process vast amounts of data.

Section 3.0 describes the foundational aspects of AI, providing you with a clear understanding of what constitutes intelligence in machines, the key elements that drive AI technologies, and a detailed explanation of the advanced fields of machine learning, deep learning, and neural networks. This comprehensive overview lays the groundwork for understanding AI's capabilities, limitations, and the potential it holds for future developments.

3.1 Understanding Intelligence: Human vs. Artificial

The comparison of human intelligence with artificial intelligence (AI) is a central theme in the study of AI. This section delves into the nature of intelligence, comparing and contrasting human cognitive abilities with those of AI systems, and exploring the complexities and nuances of both.

Defining Intelligence

Human Intelligence: Traditionally, human intelligence is characterized by abilities such as reasoning, problem-solving, learning, understanding complex ideas, emotional depth, and adapting to new situations.

Artificial Intelligence: AI, on the other hand, refers to the simulation of human intelligence processes by machines, especially computer systems. These processes include learning, reasoning, self-correction, and adapting to new inputs.

Approaches to Intelligence

The Biological Basis of Human Intelligence: Human intelligence is rooted in biological processes, particularly those occurring in the brain. It encompasses not only cognitive functions but also emotional and social intelligence.

The Computational Model of AI: AI, in contrast, is based on computational models. It involves algorithms that are designed to perform specific tasks, often by processing large amounts of data and identifying patterns.

Learning and Adaptability

Human Learning: Human beings learn from experience, using a combination of conscious and subconscious processes. This includes the ability to understand abstract concepts, apply knowledge to new situations, and learn from social interactions.

AI Learning: AI learning, primarily through machine learning algorithms, involves analyzing data, recognizing patterns, and making decisions based on that data. Unlike humans, AI typically requires large datasets to learn and does not possess intuitive understanding.

Cognitive Abilities and Limitations

Complexity in Human Thought: Humans excel at abstract thinking, creativity, and understanding context. They are capable of nuanced judgments and possess emotional intelligence.

Capabilities and Limitations of AI: AI excels in processing speed, handling large volumes of data, and performing well-defined tasks. However, it struggles with understanding context, abstract thinking, and emotional responses.

AI and Human Collaboration

Complementary Strengths: The combination of human and artificial intelligence can lead to enhanced problem-solving capabilities. AI can process and analyze data faster than humans, while humans can provide context, creativity, and ethical considerations.

The Future of Human-AI Interaction: The evolving field of AI proposes new ways for humans and AI to interact and collaborate, aiming for a synergistic relationship that leverages the strengths of both.

Summary

Understanding the differences and similarities between human and artificial intelligence is crucial in the development and application of AI technologies. While human intelligence encompasses a wide range of cognitive, emotional, and social abilities rooted in biological processes, AI focuses on simulating specific aspects of human cognition through computational models and algorithms. The strengths of AI lie in its processing power and data handling capabilities, whereas human intelligence excels in abstract thought, creativity, and emotional understanding. The future of AI development lies in creating systems that complement and augment human abilities, leading to a collaborative relationship between humans and machines. Recognizing the distinct nature of each form of intelligence is key to harnessing their potential in advancing technology and addressing complex challenges.

3.2 Key Concepts in AI: Algorithms, Data, and Learning

At the heart of Artificial Intelligence (AI) lie three fundamental concepts: algorithms, data, and learning. These components are the building blocks of AI systems and are crucial for understanding how AI functions and evolves. This section provides an in-depth look at each of these key concepts and their roles in the development and operation of AI technologies.

Algorithms: The Core of AI

Definition and Role: An algorithm in AI is a set of rules or instructions designed to solve problems or perform tasks. Algorithms are the decision-making frameworks that drive the behavior of AI systems.

Types of AI Algorithms: Includes classical algorithms like decision trees, logistic regression, and newer approaches like neural networks and deep learning models. Each type has its specific use-cases and strengths.

Data: The Fuel for AI

Importance of Data: Data is the foundational element that AI systems use to learn, make decisions, and improve over time. The quality, quantity, and relevance of data directly impact the effectiveness of AI.

Data Types and Sources: AI utilizes diverse types of data, including structured data (like databases), unstructured data (like images and text), and semi-structured data (like XML files). These data come from various sources like the internet, sensors, and organizational databases.

Learning: The Process of AI Evolution

Machine Learning: At its core, AI is about machines learning from data. Machine Learning (ML) is a subset of AI that focuses on developing algorithms capable of learning from and making predictions or decisions based on data.

Learning Methods: ML methods include supervised learning (learning with labeled data), unsupervised learning (learning from unlabeled data), and reinforcement learning (learning through trial and error).

Deep Learning: A Specialized Form of Learning

Deep Learning Explained: Deep learning is a type of machine learning that uses neural networks with many layers (deep networks) to analyze various levels of abstract data representations.

Impact of Deep Learning: Deep learning has been instrumental in achieving significant breakthroughs in areas like image and speech recognition, natural language processing, and autonomous vehicles.

Ethics and Bias in AI

The Challenge of Bias: AI systems can inherit biases present in their training data, leading to unfair or unethical outcomes.

Addressing Ethical Concerns: The AI community is actively engaged in developing methods to identify, understand, and mitigate bias in AI algorithms and datasets.

Summary

Algorithms, data, and learning are the foundational pillars of artificial intelligence. Algorithms provide the decision-making mechanisms, data acts as the crucial ingredient that fuels these algorithms, and learning is the process through which AI systems evolve and improve. Deep learning, a subset of machine learning, represents a significant advancement in the field, enabling AI systems to perform highly complex tasks. However, the growth of AI also raises important ethical considerations, particularly regarding bias and fairness. The ongoing development and refinement of AI technologies must consider these aspects to ensure the responsible and beneficial use of AI in society.

3.3 Overview of Machine Learning, Deep Learning, and Neural Networks

The realms of Machine Learning, Deep Learning, and Neural Networks represent some of the most dynamic and influential areas in Artificial Intelligence (AI). These interconnected fields have revolutionized the way machines process information and learn from data. This section offers a comprehensive overview of these concepts, their interrelations, and their impact on the development of AI.

Machine Learning: The Foundation

Definition and Scope: Machine Learning (ML) is a subset of AI that involves the development of algorithms that enable computers to learn from and make predictions or decisions based on data.

Types of Machine Learning: The main types are supervised learning (learning from labeled data), unsupervised learning (finding patterns in unlabeled data), and reinforcement learning (learning by interacting with an environment).

Key Algorithms: Important ML algorithms include linear regression, decision trees, support vector machines, and random forests, each suited for different types of problems and data sets.

Deep Learning: Advancing Machine Learning

Deep Learning Explained: Deep Learning is a subset of ML based on artificial neural networks with representation learning. It allows machines to solve complex problems by learning from large amounts of data.

Architecture of Deep Learning: Utilizes layered structures of algorithms, known as neural networks. Each layer processes an aspect of the data and passes it to the next, creating a hierarchy of learned features.

Breakthroughs and Applications: Deep Learning has led to significant advancements in fields like computer vision (image recognition), natural language processing (translation and sentiment analysis), and audio recognition.

Neural Networks: The Building Blocks

Basics of Neural Networks: Inspired by the structure and function of the human brain, neural networks consist of interconnected nodes or neurons that process and transmit information.

Types of Neural Networks: Includes feedforward neural networks (simplest type), convolutional neural networks (excellent for image processing), recurrent neural networks (ideal for sequential data like time series or language), and others.

Training Neural Networks: Involves adjusting the weights of the connections based on the error of the output compared to the expected result, typically using a method called backpropagation.

Integration and Evolution

From Data to Decision: The integration of ML, Deep Learning, and Neural Networks enables systems to transform raw data into actionable insights and decisions, learning from examples without explicit programming.

Ongoing Challenges and Research: Despite their successes, challenges such as data requirements, computational cost, interpretability, and ethical concerns remain active areas of research and development.

Summary

Machine Learning provides the foundational principles and algorithms that enable AI systems to learn from data. Deep Learning, as an extension of ML, utilizes complex neural networks to process data in a hierarchical manner, enabling remarkable progress in understanding images, text, and sounds. Neural networks, the core of Deep Learning, mimic the human brain's structure to process information in a layered and interconnected way. The synergy of these fields has led to significant advancements in AI, transforming a wide range of industries and applications. However, the rapid development of these technologies also presents ongoing challenges that need to be addressed, ensuring their responsible and effective use in solving real-world problems.

3.4 Quiz - Overview of Machine Learning, Deep Learning, and Neural Networks

Q1: Which of the following best describes artificial intelligence (AI)?

1. The ability of a computer to perform tasks that normally require human intelligence
2. The process of improving computer hardware
3. The study of biological neural networks
4. The use of mathematics to solve complex problems

Q2: What is a key difference between human intelligence and artificial intelligence?

1. AI can process information faster than human intelligence
2. Humans use electricity to think, while AI does not
3. AI is capable of emotional reasoning
4. Humans require data to learn, while AI does not

Q3: What is an algorithm in the context of artificial intelligence?

1. A device used for computing
2. A set of rules or instructions designed to solve a problem
3. A type of computer hardware
4. A database system

Q4: Why is data important in artificial intelligence?

1. It provides a source of energy for AI systems
2. It is used to train and improve AI algorithms
3. Data is not important in AI
4. It is used to make AI systems look more realistic

Q5: What is machine learning in the context of AI?

1. A process where machines develop their own hardware
2. The ability of AI systems to learn from and make decisions based on data
3. A marketing term for advanced AI
4. The study of mechanical engineering

Q6: Which of the following is NOT a type of machine learning?

1. Supervised learning
2. Unsupervised learning
3. Transductive learning
4. Reactive learning

Q7: What distinguishes deep learning from traditional machine learning?

1. Deep learning is exclusively based on linear algorithms
2. Deep learning involves neural networks with many layers
3. Deep learning does not use algorithms
4. Deep learning is another term for supervised learning

Q8: What is a neural network in the context of AI?

1. A network of computers connected to each other
2. A system that mimics the human brain to process information
3. A type of database used in AI systems
4. A tool for repairing physical neural connections in the brain

Q9: Which of the following is an application of artificial intelligence?

1. Manual record-keeping
2. Natural language processing
3. Traditional book printing
4. Non-digital art creation

Q10: How has AI evolved over time?

1. AI has remained largely the same since its inception
2. AI has evolved from simple rule-based systems to complex learning systems
3. AI has decreased in capability due to hardware limitations
4. AI has shifted focus from data processing to mechanical tasks

CHAPTER 4

Major Branches of AI

Major Branches of AI represents a comprehensive exploration of the diverse and dynamic fields within Artificial Intelligence, each contributing uniquely to the advancement of AI technologies and applications.

Machine Learning (4.1)

As a foundational pillar of AI, Machine Learning is instrumental in enabling machines to learn from data, adapt to new circumstances, and make decisions. It encompasses various algorithms and methods, including supervised, unsupervised, and reinforcement learning, and is pivotal in numerous applications ranging from predictive analytics to autonomous systems.

Natural Language Processing (NLP) (4.2)

NLP stands at the intersection of AI and linguistics, focusing on enabling machines to understand, interpret, and generate human language. This field has brought significant advancements in text and speech analysis, enabling applications such as chatbots, language translation services, and sentiment analysis, fundamentally changing how humans interact with machines.

Robotics (4.3)

Robotics integrates AI with mechanical engineering and electronics to create machines capable of performing tasks autonomously or semi-autonomously. The incorporation of AI into robotics has led to the development of more intelligent and adaptable robots, used in various domains from manufacturing to healthcare, and from personal assistance to exploration.

Computer Vision (4.4)

This branch focuses on enabling machines to interpret and process visual information from the world. Through techniques like image recognition, object detection, and deep learning models like Convolutional Neural Networks, computer vision systems have applications in areas such as facial recognition, autonomous vehicles, and medical imaging.

Expert Systems (4.5)

Expert Systems mimic the decision-making ability of human experts by using rule-based systems. Although their prominence has diminished with the rise of more advanced AI techniques, they have laid the groundwork for AI's application in complex problem-solving and continue to influence areas like medical diagnosis, financial services, and environmental control.

Overall, these branches of AI illustrate the field's breadth and depth, showcasing its impact across various industries and aspects of daily life. From machine learning's data-driven decision-making to NLP's transformation of human-computer interaction, from the versatile applications of robotics and computer vision to the specialized knowledge encapsulated in expert systems, AI continues to be a driving force in technological innovation and advancement. Each branch, with its unique focus and methodologies, contributes to the overarching goal of creating intelligent, efficient, and autonomous systems, highlighting the diverse potential of AI in addressing complex challenges and enhancing human capabilities.

We will now examine each branch in detail.

4.1 Machine Learning

Machine Learning (ML) is a pivotal and rapidly evolving field within Artificial Intelligence that focuses on developing algorithms and statistical models enabling computers to perform tasks without explicit instructions, relying instead on patterns and inference. This section delves into the core concepts, methodologies, and applications of ML, elucidating its fundamental role in modern AI.

Fundamentals of Machine Learning

- **Definition and Concept**: ML is a subset of AI where machines learn from data, identifying patterns and making decisions with minimal human intervention. It is based on the idea that systems can learn from data, identify patterns, and make decisions.
- **Key Components**: The primary components of ML include data (the raw information used for learning), algorithms (the

methods employed to process and learn from data), and models (the output or the learned representation of data).

Types of Machine Learning

- **Supervised Learning**: Involves learning a function that maps an input to an output based on example input-output pairs. It infers a function from labeled training data consisting of a set of training examples.
- **Unsupervised Learning**: Deals with how systems can infer a function to describe a hidden structure from unlabeled data. It's used to find the inherent patterns in the data.
- **Reinforcement Learning**: A method where the machine learns to behave in an environment by performing certain actions and observing the rewards/results of these actions.

Algorithms and Techniques in Machine Learning

- **Linear Regression and Logistic Regression**: Used for predicting numerical values and categorization, respectively.
- **Decision Trees and Random Forests**: Provide models for decision making and predictions, commonly used in classification and regression tasks.
- **Neural Networks**: More complex algorithms that mimic the human brain's structure and function, used in deep learning for more complex data interpretation.
- **Clustering and Dimensionality Reduction**: Techniques in unsupervised learning for grouping data and reducing the number of variables under consideration.

Applications of Machine Learning

- **Industry Applications**: From predicting consumer behavior in marketing, fraud detection in finance, to predictive maintenance in manufacturing.

- **Healthcare**: Used for disease identification and personalized medicine.
- **Technology**: Powers search engines, recommendation systems, and personal digital assistants.

Challenges and Future Directions

- **Data Quality and Quantity**: The effectiveness of ML is heavily dependent on the quality and quantity of the data used.
- **Ethical and Societal Implications**: Issues like bias in data and algorithms, privacy concerns, and the impact on employment are critical considerations.
- **Advancing Technology**: The ongoing development in areas like neural networks and reinforcement learning continues to push the boundaries of what is possible with ML.

Summary

Machine Learning stands at the forefront of AI, providing the tools and methodologies for computers to learn from data, make predictions, and improve decision-making processes. It encompasses a variety of techniques and algorithms, each suited to specific types of problems and data. ML's applications span a wide range of industries, profoundly impacting society and business practices. However, the rapid growth and capabilities of ML also present significant challenges, particularly in terms of data ethics, privacy, and the societal impact of automation. As the field continues to evolve, it holds the promise of unlocking even more sophisticated capabilities and insights, driving innovation across various domains.

4.2 Natural Language Processing (NLP)

Natural Language Processing (NLP) is a critical domain within Artificial Intelligence that focuses on the interaction between computers and human language. It involves enabling computers to understand, interpret, and generate human language in a valuable and meaningful way. This section explores the fundamentals, methodologies, applications, and challenges of NLP.

Fundamentals of Natural Language Processing

- **Definition and Scope**: NLP combines computational linguistics—rule-based modeling of human language—with statistical, machine learning, and deep learning models. The goal is to enable computers to process or "understand" natural language in order to perform tasks like translation, sentiment analysis, and more.
- **Key Components**: The core components of NLP include syntax (the arrangement of words), semantics (the meaning of words), and pragmatics (how context influences the interpretation of communication).

Major Techniques in NLP

- **Text Analysis and Tokenization**: Breaking down text into smaller units (tokens) for easier processing.
- **Part-of-Speech Tagging and Parsing**: Identifying parts of speech (nouns, verbs, etc.) and the structure of sentences.
- **Named Entity Recognition (NER)**: Identifying and categorizing key information in text (like names, places, dates).
- **Sentiment Analysis**: Determining the emotional tone behind a body of text.
- **Natural Language Generation (NLG)**: Generating human-like text from data.

Advancements in NLP

- **Machine Learning in NLP**: Use of supervised and unsupervised machine learning techniques to improve language understanding and generation.
- **Deep Learning and Neural Networks**: Implementation of deep learning models, particularly Recurrent Neural Networks (RNNs) and Transformers, for more advanced NLP tasks.

- **Language Models**: Development of sophisticated models like BERT and GPT, which have significantly advanced the field by improving the understanding of context and nuances in language.

Applications of NLP

- **Voice Assistants and Chatbots**: Enabling natural and efficient interactions between humans and machines.
- **Machine Translation**: Translating text or speech from one language to another, like in Google Translate.
- **Content Analysis and Recommendation Systems**: Analyzing user data to provide personalized content recommendations.

Challenges and Ethical Considerations

- **Dealing with Ambiguity and Context**: Natural language is inherently ambiguous and context-dependent, posing significant challenges in interpretation.
- **Bias and Fairness**: Ensuring that NLP systems are free from biases present in training data and do not perpetuate stereotypes.
- **Language Diversity**: Building NLP systems that can effectively work with a wide range of languages, including those with limited available data.

Summary

Natural Language Processing stands as a bridge between human communication and computer understanding, playing a crucial role in interpreting and generating human language. It leverages a combination of linguistic principles and advanced computational techniques, including machine learning and deep learning, to process and analyze natural language. While NLP has seen significant advancements and has a wide range of applications, it also faces unique challenges, particularly in handling the complexity, ambiguity, and diversity of human language. As technology advances, NLP continues to evolve, promising more sophisticated and nuanced language processing capabilities in the future.

4.3 Robotics

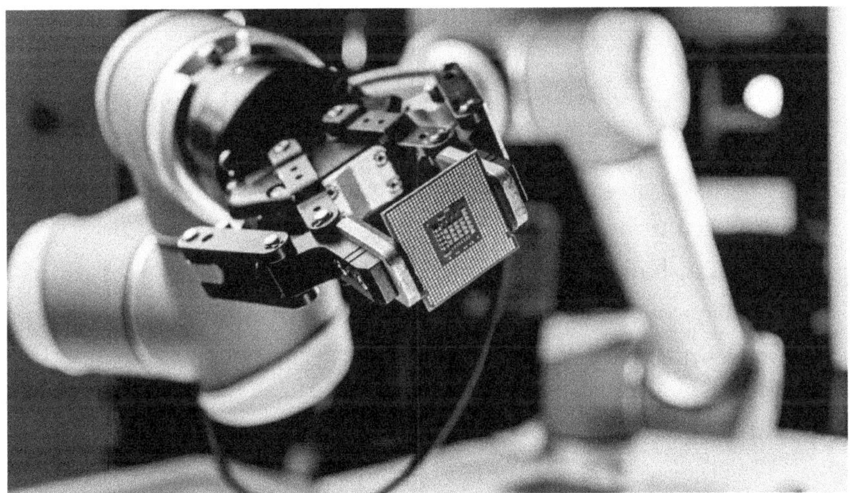

Robotics, a significant branch of Artificial Intelligence, involves the design, construction, operation, and use of robots. The integration of AI in robotics has enabled the creation of more intelligent, adaptable, and efficient machines. This section explores the intersection of robotics and AI, delving into the technologies, methodologies, applications, and challenges inherent in this dynamic field.

Fundamentals of Robotics

- **Definition and Scope**: Robotics combines engineering, computer science, and AI to create robots - machines capable of performing tasks autonomously or semi-autonomously. AI in robotics is primarily about endowing robots with intelligent decision-making capabilities.
- **Key Components**: Essential components of a robot include sensors (to perceive the environment), actuators (to interact with the

environment), and control systems (to process information and make decisions).

AI in Robotics

- **Machine Learning and Perception**: Utilizing machine learning algorithms for perception, robots can interpret and understand their environment to navigate and perform tasks more effectively.
- **Autonomous Decision Making**: AI enables robots to make decisions based on their sensory input and objectives, allowing for greater autonomy and adaptability.
- **Human-Robot Interaction**: AI-driven robotics focuses on improving interactions between humans and robots, making them more intuitive and natural.

Types of Robots

- **Industrial Robots**: Used in manufacturing for tasks like assembly, painting, and welding. These robots have revolutionized production lines by increasing efficiency and precision.
- **Service Robots**: These include domestic robots (like vacuum cleaners), medical robots (used in surgery or patient care), and public service robots (used in security or delivery services).
- **Humanoid Robots**: Designed to resemble and mimic human behavior, these robots are often used in research, education, and entertainment.

Advanced Technologies in Robotics

- **Robotics and IoT**: Integration with the Internet of Things (IoT) allows robots to share and utilize data from other devices, enhancing their functionality and application.
- **Collaborative Robots (Cobots)**: Designed to work alongside humans, cobots are used in scenarios where human-robot collaboration is beneficial.

- **Swarm Robotics**: Inspired by natural phenomena like bird flocks, these involve multiple robots working together to perform tasks, increasing efficiency and resilience.

Applications of Robotics

- **Manufacturing and Production**: Robots increase productivity, precision, and safety in manufacturing environments.
- **Healthcare**: From robotic surgery to patient rehabilitation and assistance, robots play a crucial role in modern healthcare.
- **Exploration and Research**: Robots are used in space exploration, deep-sea research, and other environments that are inaccessible or dangerous for humans.

Challenges and Future Directions

- **Technical and Ethical Challenges**: Issues include developing robust and reliable robots, ensuring safe human-robot interaction, and addressing ethical concerns like job displacement and privacy.
- **Advancing AI in Robotics**: Ongoing research aims to enhance the intelligence, autonomy, and adaptability of robots, with a focus on developing more sophisticated AI algorithms and sensor technologies.

Summary

Robotics, empowered by AI, is a field at the forefront of technological innovation, significantly impacting industries, healthcare, research, and daily life. The integration of AI in robotics has led to the development of more intelligent, flexible, and efficient machines capable of performing a wide range of tasks. While robotics has seen remarkable advancements and widespread application, it continues to face technical, ethical, and practical challenges. The future of robotics, intertwined with advancements in AI, holds the promise of even more sophisticated and integrated robotic systems, further blurring the lines between human capabilities and machine functionality.

4.4 Computer Vision

Computer Vision, a fundamental area within Artificial Intelligence, focuses on enabling machines to interpret and process visual data from the world similarly to human vision. This field encompasses the development of algorithms and systems that can detect, analyze, and understand images and videos. This section provides a comprehensive overview of computer vision, including its principles, techniques, applications, and challenges.

Principles of Computer Vision

- **Definition and Scope**: Computer Vision aims to replicate human visual perception capabilities in machines, allowing them to recognize, analyze, and interact with their environment visually.

- **Key Processes**: Includes image acquisition, processing, analysis, and understanding. The goal is for machines to extract meaningful information from visual data and make decisions based on that information.

Techniques in Computer Vision

- **Image Processing**: Basic operations like filtering, edge detection, and color processing to improve image quality or extract useful information.
- **Feature Detection and Matching**: Identifying and using specific features within images (such as edges, corners, or objects) to recognize patterns or objects.
- **Object Recognition and Classification**: Techniques to identify and classify objects within an image or video frame.
- **Deep Learning in Computer Vision**: The use of neural networks, especially Convolutional Neural Networks (CNNs), has revolutionized computer vision, enabling more accurate and efficient image recognition and classification.

Applications of Computer Vision

- **Facial Recognition**: Used in security systems, identity verification, and other personal identification applications.
- **Autonomous Vehicles**: Enables vehicles to interpret and navigate their environment.
- **Medical Image Analysis**: Assists in diagnosing diseases and analyzing medical imagery such as X-rays and MRI scans.
- **Retail and Surveillance**: Used for customer behavior analysis, security, and monitoring.

Challenges in Computer Vision

- **Variability and Quality of Visual Data**: Dealing with different lighting conditions, angles, occlusions, and image quality poses significant challenges.
- **Real-Time Processing**: Developing systems that can process and interpret visual data in real-time is critical for applications like autonomous driving.
- **Ethical and Privacy Concerns**: Especially relevant in applications like surveillance and facial recognition, where privacy and misuse are major concerns.

The Role of Data and Machine Learning

- **Training with Large Datasets**: The accuracy and effectiveness of computer vision systems depend heavily on the quantity and quality of the training data.
- **Machine Learning Models**: The advancement in ML models, particularly deep learning, has been a key driver in the progress of computer vision.

Summary

Computer Vision is an integral part of AI, aiming to replicate and enhance the human ability to interpret and understand visual data. It combines a variety of techniques from image processing to advanced machine learning, particularly deep learning, to enable machines to recognize, categorize, and interact with their visual environment. While computer vision has found diverse applications from healthcare to autonomous vehicles, it continues to face challenges related to data variability, real-time processing requirements, and ethical considerations. The ongoing advancements in AI and machine learning promise to further enhance the capabilities and applications of computer vision, making it a continually evolving and impactful field in AI.

4.5 Expert Systems

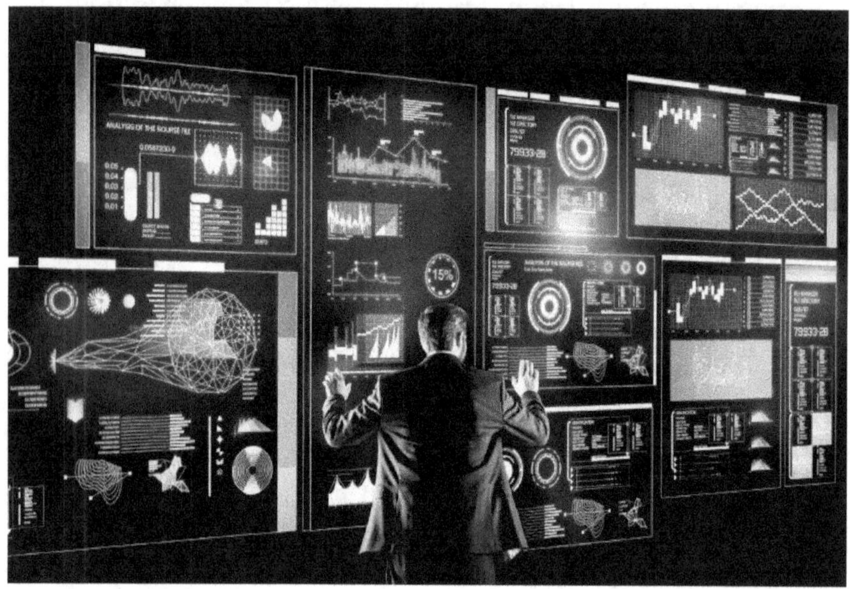

Expert Systems, a branch of Artificial Intelligence, are computer systems that emulate the decision-making ability of a human expert. They are designed to solve complex problems by reasoning through bodies of knowledge, represented primarily in the form of if-then rules rather than through conventional procedural code. This section explores the fundamentals, development, applications, and challenges of expert systems.

Fundamentals of Expert Systems

- **Definition and Characteristics**: An expert system is an AI program that uses knowledge and inference procedures to solve problems that are difficult enough to require significant human expertise for their solutions.

- **Components of Expert Systems**: Typically includes a knowledge base (containing domain-specific and high-quality knowledge), an inference engine (a mechanism that applies the knowledge to problem-solving), and a user interface (allowing interaction between the user and the system).

Development of Expert Systems

- **Knowledge Acquisition**: The process of extracting, structuring, and organizing knowledge from a domain expert to be used in the knowledge base.
- **Knowledge Representation**: Involves encoding expert knowledge and heuristics in a form that the computer can process, often using rule-based systems.
- **Inference Mechanisms**: The inference engine uses the knowledge base to draw conclusions and make decisions, often using techniques like forward chaining and backward chaining.

Applications of Expert Systems

- **Medical Diagnosis**: Assisting doctors in diagnosing diseases by analyzing symptoms, medical history, and laboratory data.
- **Financial Services**: Used for credit scoring, portfolio management, and fraud detection.
- **Manufacturing and Maintenance**: Expert systems assist in complex manufacturing processes, diagnostics, and maintenance scheduling.
- **Environmental Control**: Managing and monitoring environmental parameters in settings like greenhouses or industrial plants.

Advantages and Limitations

- **Advantages**: Include their ability to store and manipulate large amounts of specialized knowledge, making consistent decisions, and their availability for consultation at any time.
- **Limitations**: Expert systems lack common sense, cannot learn from experiences, are expensive and time-consuming to build, and can become outdated quickly if not maintained.

Current Trends and Future of Expert Systems

- **Integration with Other AI Technologies**: Combining expert systems with machine learning and data mining for enhanced performance.
- **The Decline and Transformation**: While traditional expert systems have declined, the principles and concepts are still relevant, often integrated into broader AI systems and applications.

Summary

Expert Systems represent an early and significant achievement in the field of AI, designed to encapsulate expert knowledge in a specific domain and provide decision-making assistance. They are characterized by a defined knowledge base, an efficient inference engine, and a user-friendly interface. Despite their limitations, such as the inability to learn and adapt, and the challenges in knowledge acquisition, expert systems have found applications in various fields, including medicine, finance, and manufacturing. Over time, the field of expert systems has evolved, with its principles integrating into more advanced AI systems, leveraging the advancements in machine learning and data analytics to enhance decision-making processes. The legacy of expert systems continues to influence the development of AI, contributing to the creation of more sophisticated and intelligent systems.

4.6 Quiz Major Branches of AI

Q1: Which branch of AI focuses on teaching computers to learn from and improve upon past experiences?

1. Computer Vision
2. Robotics
3. Machine Learning
4. Natural Language Processing

Q2: Natural Language Processing (NLP) is primarily concerned with:

1. Interpreting and generating human language
2. Recognizing and analyzing visual data
3. Building and programming robots
4. Creating rule-based systems for decision-making

Q3: Robotics in AI is mainly about:

1. Developing algorithms for machine learning
2. Machines that can see and interpret the world
3. Creating machines that can perform tasks autonomously
4. Analyzing large datasets

Q4: What is the main focus of Computer Vision in AI?

1. Enhancing human-computer interaction
2. Enabling machines to visually interpret the world
3. Automating manufacturing processes
4. Translating different languages

Q5: Expert Systems in AI are designed to:

1. Emulate human physical abilities

2. Mimic human decision-making expertise
3. Understand and generate natural language
4. Recognize and interpret images and videos

Q6: Which type of learning involves AI systems being trained on labeled data?

1. Unsupervised Learning
2. Supervised Learning
3. Reinforcement Learning
4. Deep Learning

Q7: In NLP, what technique is used to determine the sentiment or emotional tone behind text?

1. Object Recognition
2. Sentiment Analysis
3. Image Classification
4. Reinforcement Learning

Q8: Which AI field involves designing intelligent agents that interact with their environment?

1. Machine Learning
2. Robotics
3. Computer Vision
4. Expert Systems

Q9: Deep Learning, a subset of Machine Learning, is primarily based on:

1. Logical rules and algorithms
2. Neural networks with multiple layers
3. Language processing algorithms
4. Robotic control systems

Q10: What is a key application of Computer Vision?

1. Automated translation of languages
2. Predicting stock market trends
3. Facial recognition and image analysis
4. Rule-based problem-solving

CHAPTER 5

Tools and Technologies in AI

5.1 Programming Languages for AI (Python, R, etc.)

This subsection highlights the essential programming languages used in AI development. Python stands out for its simplicity and extensive library support, making it the most popular choice for AI and machine learning. R is particularly favored for statistical analysis and data visualization. Java offers a balance of performance and versatility, suitable for enterprise environments and big data technologies. C++ is preferred for high-performance applications, and JavaScript has become increasingly relevant for AI in web and mobile applications. Each language offers unique features and is chosen based on specific project requirements.

5.2 Frameworks and Libraries (TensorFlow, PyTorch, etc.)

Frameworks and libraries provide critical infrastructure for developing AI applications. TensorFlow, developed by Google, is renowned for its flexible architecture and is widely used in both research and production. PyTorch, known for its simplicity and dynamic computation graph, is favored in the research community. Scikit-learn is a primary choice for classical machine learning tasks, while Keras facilitates easy and fast prototyping of deep learning models. Other notable frameworks include Apache MXNet and Caffe, each contributing uniquely to the AI development process.

5.3 Hardware for AI (GPUs, TPUs, etc.)

The hardware used in AI significantly impacts the performance and efficiency of AI applications. GPUs are crucial for parallel processing tasks in deep learning and data-intensive AI tasks. Google's TPUs offer specialized high-performance processing for neural network machine learning. FPGAs provide a flexible hardware solution, customizable for specific AI applications, and modern CPUs are increasingly capable of handling AI tasks more efficiently. The choice of hardware is a key consideration in AI projects, depending on the specific needs of the application.

The tools and technologies used in AI, from programming languages to frameworks, libraries, and hardware, are integral to the development and success of AI applications. They each bring distinct advantages and cater to different aspects of AI development, from data processing and model building to efficient computation and deployment. The continuous evolution and improvement of these tools and technologies are critical in driving forward the capabilities and applications of AI.

5.1 Programming Languages for AI (Python, R, etc.)

The choice of programming languages is pivotal in the development and implementation of Artificial Intelligence (AI) technologies. Different languages offer various features and libraries that cater to the diverse needs of AI projects, from data analysis to neural network implementation. This section highlights the most prominent programming languages used in AI, focusing on their characteristics, strengths, and typical applications.

Python: The Leading Language in AI

Overview: Python's simplicity, flexibility, and robust library ecosystem make it the most popular language for AI and machine learning projects.

Key Libraries: Libraries like TensorFlow, PyTorch, Scikit-learn, and Keras facilitate various AI and machine learning tasks.

Applications: Widely used in data analysis, machine learning, deep learning, and natural language processing.

R: The Statistician's Choice

Overview: R is particularly favored for statistical analysis and data visualization, making it a strong choice for AI applications involving complex statistical computations.

Key Libraries: Packages like ggplot2 for data visualization and caret for machine learning are widely used.

Applications: Predominantly used in academia and research for statistical analysis, bioinformatics, and econometrics.

Java: Balancing Performance and Versatility

Overview: Java's portability, ease of debugging, and efficient memory management make it a strong contender for developing scalable AI applications.

Key Libraries: Libraries like Weka, Deeplearning4j, and MOA support machine learning and data mining.

Applications: Often used in enterprise environments, web applications, and big data technologies.

C++: For Performance-Critical AI Systems

Overview: C++ is known for its high-performance capabilities, making it suitable for AI projects where speed and resource management are critical.

Key Libraries: Libraries such as Shark and MLpack cater to machine learning and data processing needs.

Applications: Used in game development, real-time systems, and applications where hardware interaction is crucial.

JavaScript: AI in Web and Mobile Applications

Overview: With the rise of Node.js, JavaScript has become a viable option for AI implementations in web and mobile app development.

Key Libraries: TensorFlow.js allows the integration of machine learning in web applications.

Applications: Ideal for developing interactive AI-driven web and mobile applications.

Other Notable Languages

Julia: Known for high-performance numerical computing, increasingly used in machine learning and AI research.

Lisp: One of the earliest programming languages used in AI, favored for its prototyping capabilities but less common in modern applications.

Summary

In the realm of AI development, the choice of programming language can significantly influence the efficiency and effectiveness of the solution. Python stands out for its simplicity and extensive libraries, making it a top choice for a wide range of AI applications. R excels in statistical analysis, while Java offers a balance between performance and versatility, and C++ is preferred for performance-critical applications. JavaScript's role in AI is growing, particularly in web and mobile domains. Other languages like Julia and Lisp also contribute uniquely to the field. Each language brings distinct advantages and is chosen based on the specific requirements and objectives of the AI project, demonstrating the diversity and dynamism in AI development tools.

5.2 Frameworks and Libraries (TensorFlow, PyTorch, etc.)

Frameworks and libraries are fundamental tools in the development of Artificial Intelligence (AI) and Machine Learning (ML) projects. They provide pre-written code, algorithms, and functions that simplify the implementation of complex tasks in AI. This section delves into some of the most widely used frameworks and libraries in AI, discussing their features, strengths, and typical use cases.

TensorFlow: Google's Open-Source Framework

Overview: Developed by the Google Brain team, TensorFlow is an open-source library for numerical computation and machine learning.

Key Features: Offers flexible architecture for deploying computation across various platforms (CPUs, GPUs, TPUs), extensive toolkits for deep learning, and a visualization tool called TensorBoard.

Applications: Widely used in both research and production for tasks like image and speech recognition, natural language processing, and predictive analytics.

PyTorch: Preferred for Research and Development

Overview: Developed by Facebook's AI Research lab, PyTorch is known for its simplicity, ease of use, and dynamic computation graph.

Key Features: Supports tensor computation with strong GPU acceleration and dynamic neural networks, which are particularly useful in research and prototyping.

Applications: Popular among researchers for its flexibility and ease of experimentation, especially in deep learning and neural network projects.

Scikit-learn: For Classical Machine Learning

Overview: Built on NumPy, SciPy, and matplotlib, scikit-learn is a Python library for classical machine learning.

Key Features: Includes simple and efficient tools for data mining and data analysis, with a broad range of algorithms for classification, regression, clustering, and dimensionality reduction.

Applications: Ideal for standard machine learning and data analysis tasks, particularly in scenarios where deep learning is not required.

Keras: High-Level Neural Networks API

Overview: Keras, now integrated with TensorFlow, is a high-level neural networks API, known for its user-friendliness and modularity.

Key Features: Allows for easy and fast prototyping, supports both convolutional networks and recurrent networks, and works seamlessly on both CPUs and GPUs.

Applications: Used for building and training deep learning models with an emphasis on enabling fast experimentation.

Other Notable Frameworks and Libraries

Apache MXNet: Supported by Amazon, it's known for its efficiency in scaling across multiple GPUs and machines.

Theano: An older library, it paved the way for many other frameworks but is now less commonly used.

Caffe/Caffe2: Preferred for image classification and convolutional neural networks, with speed being its major advantage.

Summary

Frameworks and libraries like TensorFlow, PyTorch, Scikit-learn, and Keras are integral to AI and ML development, each offering unique features and specializations. TensorFlow stands out for its scalability and extensive toolkits, PyTorch is favored in research due to its flexibility, Scikit-learn excels in classical machine learning tasks, and Keras simplifies deep learning model building. Other frameworks like MXNet and Caffe also play significant roles in specific applications. The choice of a framework or library depends on the specific requirements of the project, such as the complexity of the task, the need for speed and efficiency, and the level of expertise required. These tools not only streamline the development process but also continually evolve, pushing the boundaries of what's possible in AI and ML.

5.3 Hardware for AI (GPUs, TPUs, etc.)

The rapid advancement of Artificial Intelligence (AI) and Machine Learning (ML) technologies has been significantly supported by parallel developments in hardware. Specialized hardware like GPUs (Graphics Processing Units) and TPUs (Tensor Processing Units) play a critical role in efficiently processing the vast amounts of data required for AI applications. This section discusses the key hardware components used in AI, their features, and their importance.

GPUs: The Workhorse of AI and Deep Learning

Overview: Initially designed for rendering graphics in video games, GPUs have become a cornerstone in AI due to their ability to perform parallel operations on large blocks of data, making them ideal for deep learning algorithms.

Key Features: GPUs offer high computational power and parallelism, which are essential for training complex neural networks and processing large datasets.

Applications: Widely used in deep learning, computer vision, natural language processing, and other data-intensive AI tasks.

TPUs: Google's Specialized AI Hardware

Overview: Developed by Google, TPUs are application-specific integrated circuits (ASICs) designed specifically for neural network machine learning.

Key Features: TPUs are optimized for TensorFlow, Google's open-source machine learning framework, and are designed to accelerate both the training and inference phases of deep neural networks.

Applications: Used primarily in Google's large data centers for applications like Google Search, Google Photos, and in products that require complex neural network computations.

FPGAs: Flexible Hardware for Custom AI Solutions

Overview: Field-Programmable Gate Arrays (FPGAs) are semiconductor devices that are based around a matrix of configurable logic blocks (CLBs) connected via programmable interconnects.

Key Features: FPGAs can be reprogrammed to desired application or functionality requirements after manufacturing, offering a versatile and customizable hardware solution for AI applications.

*Applications**: Ideal for specific AI tasks where custom hardware configurations can lead to performance improvements, such as in edge computing scenarios.

CPUs: Traditional but Evolving

Overview: Central Processing Units (CPUs) are the general-purpose processors found in most computers. While they are not as fast as GPUs or TPUs for parallel processing tasks, recent advancements have made them more viable for certain AI applications.

Key Features: Modern CPUs are becoming more efficient at handling AI tasks, especially with improvements in multi-threading and integration of AI-specific instructions. - **Applications**: Suitable for AI applications that don't require intense parallel processing or can benefit from the CPU's versatility in handling diverse tasks.

Emerging Technologies

Quantum Computing: An emerging field that, in the future, could revolutionize the processing capabilities for certain types of AI problems, particularly in optimization and simulation.

Summary

The landscape of AI hardware is diverse, with GPUs, TPUs, FPGAs, and modern CPUs each playing a unique role in the field. GPUs are widely recognized for their parallel processing capabilities, making them ideal for training deep learning models. TPUs offer specialized, high-performance processing for neural network-related tasks, particularly in large-scale environments. FPGAs provide flexibility and customization for specific AI applications, while CPUs remain a versatile, though less specialized, option. As AI continues to evolve, the development of hardware tailored to AI's unique computational needs is expected to advance, offering even greater performance and efficiency for AI applications.

CHAPTER 6

Ethics and Challenges in AI

Ethics and Challenges in AI delves into the critical ethical considerations and challenges arising from the rapid advancement and integration of Artificial Intelligence (AI) in various sectors.

Ethical Considerations in AI Development (6.1)

This subsection emphasizes the importance of ethical design and use of AI systems. Key issues include ensuring AI respects human rights and values, mitigating biases in AI algorithms and datasets, promoting transparency and explainability in AI decisions, and balancing technological advancements with societal and ethical implications. Ethical AI development involves considering the broader impact of AI on society, including potential changes in employment, societal structures, and human interactions.

Bias and Fairness in AI Systems (6.2)

This part focuses on the challenges of bias and fairness in AI. It highlights how biases in data and algorithms can lead to unfair and discriminatory outcomes. Strategies to combat AI bias include diversifying datasets, implementing fairness-aware algorithms, and continuous monitoring for biased outcomes. The section also discusses the importance of measuring and testing for bias, as well as the societal and economic implications of biased AI systems.

Privacy and Security Concerns (6.3)

Addressing privacy and security in the context of AI, this subsection explores the privacy challenges related to the collection and use of large datasets, including personal and sensitive information. It also examines the security risks inherent in AI systems, such as vulnerability to cyber-attacks and the potential misuse of AI in cybersecurity. Strategies for ensuring privacy and security are discussed, including privacy by design, robust security measures, and adherence to regulatory and ethical frameworks.

Section 6.0 underlines the imperative of addressing ethical issues, biases, privacy, and security concerns in AI development and deployment. It underscores the need for a comprehensive and proactive approach that includes technical solutions, regulatory compliance, and ethical considerations. As AI technologies continue to evolve and permeate various aspects of life, these challenges must be continually addressed to ensure responsible, fair, and secure use of AI.

6.1 Ethical Considerations in AI Development

Introduction

As Artificial Intelligence (AI) increasingly influences various aspects of society, ethical considerations in its development and deployment have become paramount. Ethical AI involves the design and use of AI systems in a manner that respects human rights and values. This section explores key ethical concerns in AI, including bias, transparency, accountability, and the societal impact of AI technologies.

Bias and Fairness

Data and Algorithmic Bias: AI systems can inadvertently perpetuate and amplify societal biases present in their training data, leading to unfair outcomes.

Mitigating Bias: Efforts include diversifying data sets, implementing fairness-aware algorithms, and continuous monitoring for biased outcomes.

Transparency and Explainability

The Black Box Problem: Many AI systems, particularly deep learning models, are often seen as 'black boxes' due to their complex and opaque decision-making processes.

Promoting Transparency: Developing AI with explainable and interpretable models is crucial for users to understand, trust, and effectively manage AI decisions.

Accountability and Responsibility

Assigning Responsibility: Determining responsibility for AI decisions, especially when they lead to unintended or harmful outcomes, is challenging.

Legal and Ethical Accountability: Establishing clear guidelines and legal frameworks for AI accountability is essential, including who is responsible for the development and deployment of AI systems.

Privacy and Surveillance

Data Privacy: AI's reliance on large data sets raises concerns about privacy and data protection.

Balancing Act: Ensuring AI systems respect individual privacy rights, while leveraging data for beneficial purposes, is a significant ethical challenge.

Societal Impact

Job Displacement: AI and automation could lead to significant shifts in employment, raising concerns about job security and economic inequality.

Social Well-being: The broad impact of AI on social structures, including potential changes in human behavior and interaction, necessitates careful consideration.

Global Ethics in AI

Cultural Differences: Ethical AI development must consider cultural and contextual differences globally, avoiding a one-size-fits-all approach.

International Collaboration: Collaboration among countries, industries, and academia is crucial to develop globally acceptable ethical AI standards.

Summary

Ethical considerations in AI development are crucial to ensure that AI technologies are used in a way that is beneficial, fair, and respects human rights. Addressing issues such as bias and fairness, transparency, accountability, privacy, and the societal impact of AI is essential for building trust and acceptance of AI systems. As the field of AI continues to evolve, ethical considerations must be integrated into every stage of AI development, from design to deployment. This includes not only technical solutions but also robust legal and regulatory frameworks, ongoing public dialogue, and international collaboration to navigate the complex ethical landscape of AI.

6.2 Bias and Fairness in AI Systems

Bias and fairness in AI systems have become critical topics as these systems increasingly influence various aspects of our lives, from job screening to judicial decisions. AI bias refers to systematic and unfair discrimination in the outputs of AI systems. This section delves into the causes, implications, and strategies to mitigate bias and ensure fairness in AI.

Understanding AI Bias

Sources of Bias: AI bias often originates from biased training data, biased algorithms, or a combination of both. Biases in data can arise from historical inequalities or unrepresentative data samples.

Types of Bias: Includes sampling bias, measurement bias, algorithmic bias, and cultural bias. Each type affects the AI's decision-making process, leading to skewed or unfair outcomes.

Impacts of AI Bias

Societal Implications:

Biased AI systems can reinforce existing social biases, leading to unfair treatment of certain groups, especially in critical areas like hiring, lending, and law enforcement.

Economic Consequences: Unfair AI systems can result in economic disadvantages for affected groups and might lead to legal repercussions for organizations that use them.

Measuring and Testing for Bias

Fairness Metrics: Various metrics and frameworks have been developed to measure bias and fairness in AI systems, such as demographic parity, equality of opportunity, and individual fairness.

Testing Methods: Implementing rigorous testing regimes, including both technical analysis and human review, is crucial for detecting and understanding bias in AI models.

Strategies for Mitigating Bias

Diversifying Training Data: Ensuring training datasets are diverse and representative of the population helps reduce the risk of biased outcomes.

Algorithmic Fairness Techniques: Techniques like reweighing training data, using fairness-aware algorithms, and model regularization can help mitigate bias.

Continuous Monitoring and Updating: Regularly monitoring AI systems post-deployment is essential to identify and rectify emerging biases over time.

Ethical and Legal Considerations

Ethical Frameworks: Developing AI within ethical frameworks that prioritize fairness is vital. This includes involving diverse teams in the development process and considering the societal impact of AI systems.

Legal Compliance: Adhering to existing and emerging laws and regulations related to AI and non-discrimination is critical for organizations.

Summary

Bias and fairness in AI systems are complex challenges that require a multifaceted approach, including technical, ethical, and legal considerations. The source of AI bias is often rooted in the data or algorithms used, leading to systemic and unfair outcomes. Mitigating bias involves careful attention to the diversity of training data, application of fairness-aware techniques, continuous monitoring, and adherence to ethical and legal standards. As AI systems become more prevalent in decision-making processes, ensuring their fairness and unbiased nature is not just a technical necessity but also a moral and legal imperative. This commitment to fairness in AI will help build trust and ensure the equitable use of AI technologies across all sectors of society.

6.3 Privacy and Security Concerns

The integration of Artificial Intelligence (AI) into various aspects of our lives raises significant privacy and security concerns. AI systems often rely on vast amounts of data, some of which are sensitive or personal. Moreover, the increasing sophistication of AI poses new security challenges. This section examines the privacy and security implications associated with AI technologies and suggests ways to address these critical issues.

Privacy Concerns in AI

Data Collection and Usage: AI systems require large datasets for training and operation, which often include personal data. The collection, storage, and use of this data raise concerns about individual privacy.

Consent and Transparency: Issues arise regarding how data is collected and used, and whether individuals are aware of or have consented to their data being used for AI purposes.

Data Anonymization and De-identification: While techniques exist to anonymize data, they are not foolproof. Sophisticated AI algorithms can sometimes re-identify anonymized data.

Security Risks in AI Systems

Vulnerability to Attacks: AI systems, like any software, are vulnerable to cyberattacks. These can include data poisoning, model stealing, and adversarial attacks designed to trick AI models.

AI in Cybersecurity: While AI can enhance cybersecurity efforts, malicious use of AI could lead to more sophisticated cyberattacks.

Regulatory and Ethical Frameworks

Data Protection Regulations: Laws like the General Data Protection Regulation (GDPR) in the EU provide guidelines and restrictions on data collection and usage, which directly impact AI development.

Ethical Guidelines for AI: Developing and implementing ethical guidelines for AI use can help address privacy concerns.

Strategies for Ensuring Privacy and Security

Privacy by Design: Incorporating privacy considerations into the design phase of AI development, ensuring that privacy protection is an integral part of the system.

Robust Security Measures: Implementing strong security protocols and constantly updating them to protect AI systems from evolving threats.

Transparency and Accountability: Providing clear information about how AI systems use data and establishing accountability mechanisms for data misuse.

Summary

Privacy and security are paramount concerns in the development and deployment of AI systems. The extensive data requirements for AI pose significant privacy challenges, while the complexity and capabilities of AI systems introduce new security vulnerabilities. Addressing these issues requires a combination of robust technical solutions, regulatory compliance, ethical considerations, and continuous vigilance. Ensuring privacy and security in AI is not just a technical requirement but also a fundamental aspect of building trust and credibility in AI technologies, essential for their sustainable and responsible use in society.

6.4 Quiz - Ethics and Challenges in AI

Q1: What is a primary ethical consideration in AI development?

1. Maximizing profit margins
2. Ensuring AI systems are entertaining
3. Making AI systems as complex as possible
4. Ensuring AI systems do not cause harm

Q2: Why is it important to consider the societal impact of AI?

1. It is important only for marketing purposes
2. AI can have significant effects on employment, privacy, and fairness
3. Society has little influence on AI development
4. AI development does not impact society

Q3: What causes bias in AI systems?

1. Bias in AI systems is always intentional
2. Biased data used in training the AI
3. AI systems are inherently unbiased
4. Bias is only caused by hardware malfunctions

Q4: How can fairness be promoted in AI systems?

1. By ignoring the data
2. By using only one type of algorithm
3. By ensuring diverse and representative data
4. Fairness is not a concern in AI

Q5: Why is privacy a concern in AI?

1. AI systems do not affect privacy
2. AI can process and store large amounts of personal data
3. Privacy concerns are only relevant for social media
4. AI systems are incapable of accessing private data

Q6: What is a security risk associated with AI?

1. AI systems cannot be hacked
2. AI always improves security
3. Vulnerability to cyber attacks and data breaches
4. AI systems are too simple to pose security risks

Q7: Who should be held accountable for decisions made by AI systems?

1. Only the AI system itself
2. The developers and organizations behind the AI systems
3. AI systems do not make decisions
4. Accountability is not applicable to AI

Q8: Why is transparency important in AI systems?

1. It is only important for aesthetic reasons
2. Transparency helps build trust and allows for better understanding of AI decisions
3. AI systems are naturally transparent
4. Transparency has no impact on AI

Q9: How can AI impact human rights?

1. AI has no impact on human rights
2. By potentially affecting privacy, freedom of expression, and non-discrimination
3. Human rights are a concern only for manual processes
4. AI improves human rights by default

Q10: What is a method to mitigate bias in AI systems?

1. Using the same data for every AI system
2. Ignoring user feedback
3. Regularly reviewing and updating datasets and algorithms
4. Bias cannot be mitigated in AI systems

CHAPTER 7

AI in Practice

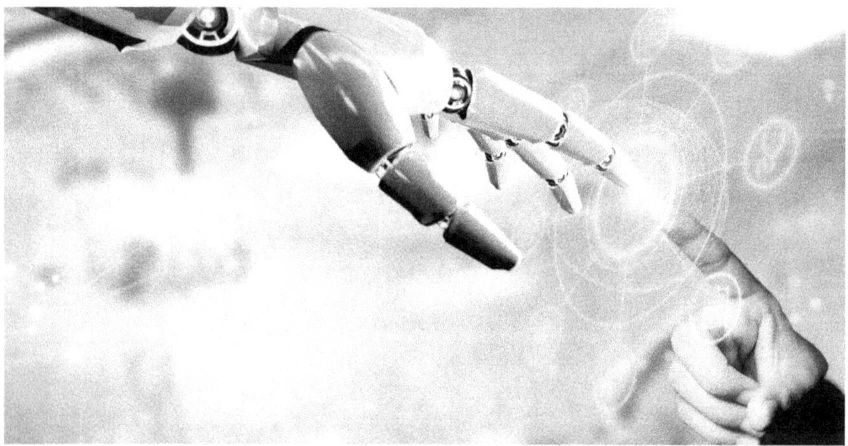

AI in Practice delves into the practical aspects of Artificial Intelligence (AI), highlighting its real-world applications, industry-specific case studies, and the implications for employment in an AI-driven future.

Real-World Applications of AI (7.1)

This subsection explores the diverse and expansive applications of AI across various fields. It covers how AI is being used in healthcare for diagnostics and treatment planning, in finance for fraud detection and algorithmic trading, in transportation for autonomous vehicles, in retail for personalized customer experiences, and in many other sectors. The section emphasizes the transformative impact of AI technologies in solving complex problems and enhancing efficiency and productivity in numerous domains.

Case Studies from Various Industries (7.2)

This part presents detailed case studies demonstrating the implementation and impact of AI in different industries. These studies provide insights into how AI is being integrated into business processes, its role in driving innovation, and the tangible benefits it offers, such as improved accuracy, cost reduction, and decision-making enhancements. The case studies range from AI in manufacturing and supply chain optimization to AI in entertainment and content creation, offering a comprehensive view of AI's versatile applications.

The Future of Employment in an AI World (7.3)

This subsection addresses one of the most critical aspects of AI's impact on society: the future of employment. It discusses how AI is expected to transform job markets, with automation potentially displacing certain jobs while simultaneously creating new opportunities in emerging fields. The section explores the need for workforce reskilling and upskilling, the evolving nature of job roles in an AI-integrated workplace, and the broader economic implications of AI on labor markets. The importance of preparing for a future where AI plays a significant role in the workforce is underscored.

*Section 7.0 AI in Practice presents a comprehensive overview of how AI is being applied in the real world, offering a glimpse into its diverse applications across industries and its profound impact on the future of employment. By showcasing practical implementations and exploring future employment trends, this section illustrates the significant role AI is poised to play in shaping various aspects of our lives and the global economy.

7.1 Real-World Applications of AI

Artificial Intelligence (AI) has transitioned from a field of theoretical research to a practical technology with widespread applications in various sectors of society. The real-world applications of AI are diverse, touching upon numerous industries and changing the way tasks are approached and solved. This section explores some of the key areas where AI has made a significant impact.

Healthcare

Disease Diagnosis and Predictive Analytics: AI algorithms can analyze medical images, detect abnormalities, and assist in early disease diagnosis, such as cancer or diabetic retinopathy. Predictive analytics can identify patients at risk and help in preventive care.

Drug Discovery and Personalized Medicine: AI accelerates the drug development process and tailors medical treatments to individual patients, improving treatment effectiveness.

Finance

Algorithmic Trading: AI systems analyze market trends and execute trades at high speeds, optimizing investment strategies.

Fraud Detection and Risk Management: AI can identify unusual patterns indicative of fraudulent activities and assess credit risk with greater accuracy than traditional methods.

Retail and E-Commerce

Personalized Recommendations: AI algorithms analyze consumer behavior to provide personalized product recommendations, enhancing the shopping experience.

Inventory and Supply Chain Management: AI optimizes inventory levels and improves supply chain efficiency by predicting demand and identifying potential disruptions.

Transportation and Autonomous Vehicles

Self-driving Cars: AI is integral to the development of autonomous vehicles, handling tasks like environment perception, decision-making, and navigation.

Traffic Management: AI optimizes traffic flow, reduces congestion, and enhances public transportation systems.

Manufacturing

Predictive Maintenance: AI predicts equipment failures before they occur, reducing downtime and maintenance costs.

Automation and Quality Control: AI-driven robots automate repetitive tasks and improve quality control through precise inspection.

Agriculture

Crop Monitoring and Analysis: AI-driven drones and sensors monitor crop health, optimize agricultural practices, and increase yield.

Precision Farming: AI enables farmers to make data-driven decisions, enhancing productivity and sustainability.

Entertainment

Content Recommendation: Streaming services like Netflix use AI to recommend movies and shows based on user preferences.

Game Development: AI enhances the gaming experience by creating more realistic and responsive environments.

Education

Personalized Learning: AI tailors educational content to students' learning styles and needs, making education more effective and engaging.

Automation of Administrative Tasks: AI automates grading and administrative tasks, allowing educators to focus more on teaching.

Summary

The real-world applications of AI are vast and growing, profoundly impacting industries such as healthcare, finance, retail, transportation, manufacturing, agriculture, entertainment, and education. AI's capabilities to analyze large datasets, automate complex processes, and provide insights are driving efficiency, innovation, and improved services across these sectors. As AI continues to evolve, its applications are likely to expand further, offering new solutions to complex challenges and transforming the way we live and work.

7.2 Case Studies from Various Industries

Introduction

The implementation of Artificial Intelligence (AI) across different industries provides a window into its transformative capabilities. Examining specific case studies from various sectors illustrates how AI is being leveraged to solve unique challenges, optimize operations, and create new opportunities. This section delves into a series of case studies showcasing AI's impact in diverse fields.

Healthcare: AI in Diagnosing Diseases

- **Case Study: Radiology Imaging Analysis**
  - An AI system was implemented to analyze radiology images for faster and more accurate diagnosis of diseases such as cancer.
  - The AI model significantly reduced diagnosis time and improved detection rates, assisting radiologists in identifying subtle abnormalities that might be overlooked.

Finance: AI in Fraud Detection

- **Case Study: AI in Credit Card Fraud Prevention**
  - A financial institution employed AI to analyze transaction patterns and detect fraudulent activities.
  - The AI system was able to identify unusual patterns and flag potential frauds, reducing false positives and minimizing financial losses.

Retail: AI for Personalized Shopping Experiences

- **Case Study: AI in Online Retail**
  - An online retailer implemented an AI-powered recommendation engine to personalize the shopping experience.

- ◦ The system analyzed browsing and purchase history, significantly increasing sales by recommending relevant products to customers.

Manufacturing: AI in Predictive Maintenance

- **Case Study: AI in Automotive Manufacturing**
  - ◦ An automotive manufacturer used AI to predict equipment failures and schedule maintenance.
  - ◦ The AI system analyzed data from sensors on equipment, reducing downtime and maintenance costs by preemptively addressing issues.

Agriculture: AI for Crop Yield Optimization

- **Case Study: AI in Precision Farming**
  - ◦ A farming operation utilized AI to analyze soil conditions, weather data, and crop health to optimize farming practices.
  - ◦ The AI application led to an increase in crop yields and more efficient resource usage, enhancing overall farm productivity.

Transportation: AI in Traffic Management

- **Case Study: AI for Urban Traffic Control**
  - ◦ A city implemented an AI system to manage traffic flow, reducing congestion and improving public transportation.
  - ◦ The AI analyzed traffic patterns in real-time, optimizing traffic light timings and reducing commute times.

Education: AI for Personalized Learning

- **Case Study: AI in Language Learning Platforms**

- ○ An AI-driven language learning platform offered personalized learning experiences based on user proficiency and learning style.
- ○ The platform adapted content and difficulty in real-time, improving language learning outcomes for users.

Summary

These case studies from various industries demonstrate the versatile and transformative nature of AI. In healthcare, AI aids in faster and more accurate disease diagnosis. In finance, it enhances fraud detection capabilities. AI revolutionizes the retail experience through personalized recommendations, optimizes manufacturing processes through predictive maintenance, increases agricultural yields with precision farming, manages urban traffic flow more efficiently, and personalizes education to enhance learning. Each case study underscores the potential of AI to not only improve operational efficiencies but also to innovate and redefine industry practices.

7.3 The Future of Employment in an AI World

The advent of Artificial Intelligence (AI) is reshaping the landscape of employment, bringing both challenges and opportunities. While AI's automation capabilities may displace certain jobs, they also pave the way for new types of employment and demand for new skills. This section explores how the rise of AI is likely to impact the future job market and the nature of work itself.

Automation and Job Displacement

Impact on Routine Jobs: AI and automation are expected to most significantly impact jobs involving routine, repetitive tasks, which are more easily automated. This includes roles in manufacturing, data entry, and some aspects of customer service.

Higher Demand for Technical Skills: There will be an increased demand for workers skilled in AI, data science, and related technological fields.

Creation of New Job Categories

Emergence of New Roles: AI will create new job categories, particularly in AI development, maintenance, and oversight. Roles like AI trainers, ethicists, and data annotators are emerging.

Evolution of Existing Roles: Existing jobs will evolve, integrating AI tools to enhance productivity and efficiency. For example, doctors will use AI for diagnostic assistance, and marketers will leverage AI for personalized advertising.

Shift in Skill Requirements

Upskilling and Reskilling: The workforce will need to adapt to the changing job landscape, requiring upskilling or reskilling, especially in AI and digital literacy.

Soft Skills Emphasis: AI is less likely to replicate human soft skills like creativity, emotional intelligence, and complex problem-solving, increasing the value of these skills in the job market.

Ethical and Social Implications

Impact on Employment Patterns: The potential for significant job displacement raises concerns about unemployment rates, income inequality, and social stability.

Need for Policy Interventions: Governments and organizations may need to develop policies to manage the transition, such as education and training programs, social safety nets, and regulations around AI and employment.

Long-Term Outlook

Collaborative Human-AI Workforce: The future is likely to see a hybrid workforce where humans and AI systems collaborate, with AI handling routine tasks and humans focusing on complex and creative tasks.

Continuous Adaptation: The job market will continually evolve, requiring a flexible and adaptable workforce and ongoing learning and development.

Summary

The integration of AI into the workplace is a double-edged sword, presenting challenges in the form of job displacement and automation, while also creating new opportunities through the emergence of novel roles and the transformation of existing ones. The future of employment in an AI world will be characterized by a shift in skill requirements, with an increased emphasis on both technical skills and soft skills. Adapting to this changing landscape requires concerted efforts in education, policy-making, and workforce development. The long-term success in this AI-driven era will hinge on our ability to leverage AI's strengths while nurturing the uniquely human capabilities that AI cannot replicate.

CHAPTER 8

The Future of AI

The Future of AI provides an insightful exploration into the prospective advancements and directions of Artificial Intelligence (AI), focusing on emerging trends, the concept of Artificial General Intelligence (AGI), and various predictions about the future of AI.

Emerging Trends in AI (8.1)

This subsection discusses the latest developments and emerging trends in the field of AI. It highlights the integration of AI with quantum computing, which promises to enhance computational power significantly, enabling AI systems to solve complex problems more efficiently. The impact of AI in healthcare is also explored, illustrating how AI is revolutionizing diagnostics, treatment planning, and patient care through advanced analytics and machine learning techniques.

The Road to Artificial General Intelligence (AGI) (8.2)

AGI, or the development of AI systems with generalized human cognitive abilities, is presented as the next significant milestone in AI evolution. This part delves into the ongoing research and the challenges faced in achieving AGI, such as developing AI that can understand, learn, and apply knowledge across a wide range of tasks and disciplines, much like a human brain.

Predictions and Speculations about AI's Future (8.3)

The final subsection offers predictions and speculations about the future trajectory of AI. It discusses the potential societal, economic, and ethical implications of advanced AI systems. The prospects of AI enhancing or disrupting various sectors, the balance between AI's benefits and risks, and the ethical considerations of advanced AI deployments are all explored to give a comprehensive view of what the future might hold.

Section 8.0 of the book provides a forward-looking perspective on AI, highlighting the rapid advancements in the field and its integration into various domains. From the potential of quantum computing to revolutionize AI processing capabilities to the ambitious goals of achieving AGI, this section paints a picture of a future where AI's influence permeates even deeper into our lives and global systems. It also responsibly acknowledges the challenges and ethical considerations that come with such advancements, underscoring the need for careful and thoughtful navigation of the AI landscape in the years to come.

8.1 Emerging Trends in AI (Quantum Computing, AI in Healthcare)

The landscape of Artificial Intelligence (AI) is rapidly evolving, with groundbreaking trends emerging that redefine its capabilities and applications. Two of the most significant trends are the integration of AI with Quantum Computing and the application of AI in Healthcare. This section delves deeply into these trends, examining their current state, future potential, and the challenges they bring.

Quantum Computing and AI

The Convergence of Quantum Computing and AI: Quantum Computing utilizes the principles of quantum mechanics to process information, offering processing power far beyond traditional computing. This convergence has the potential to revolutionize AI by providing immense computational resources to solve complex problems. **Implications for AI Algorithms**: Quantum Computing can significantly accelerate machine learning algorithms, particularly those involving large-scale optimization problems and simulations. It could enable AI to analyze vast datasets more efficiently, leading to more accurate models and predictions. - **Challenges and Future Potential**: Building stable and scalable quantum computers remains a technical challenge. The development of quantum algorithms tailored for AI applications is an ongoing area of research. The full potential of quantum computing in AI is yet to be realized, but it holds promise for solving some of AI's most computationally intensive problems.

AI in Healthcare

Transforming Diagnostics and Treatment

AI's impact on healthcare is profound, especially in diagnostics. Machine learning algorithms can process and analyze medical images with higher accuracy and speed than traditional methods, aiding in early and more precise disease diagnosis. AI is also instrumental in developing personalized treatment plans based on patient-specific data, leading to more effective healthcare interventions.

Accelerating Drug Discovery

AI is streamlining the drug discovery process, from identifying potential drug candidates to predicting their effectiveness and side effects. Machine learning models can analyze biological and chemical data to uncover new drug candidates faster than traditional methods.

Ethical and Privacy Concerns

The application of AI in healthcare raises significant ethical issues, including patient data privacy, security, and the risk of AI systems inheriting biases from training data. Ensuring that AI systems in healthcare are fair, transparent, and privacy-compliant is crucial.

Summary

The emerging trends of Quantum Computing and AI in Healthcare are at the forefront of AI's evolution. Quantum computing promises to provide the computational power necessary to propel AI into new frontiers, potentially solving complex problems that are currently beyond reach. In healthcare, AI is already making significant strides in improving diagnostics, personalizing treatment, and accelerating drug discovery, though it faces challenges related to ethics and data privacy. As these trends progress, they are set to profoundly impact not only the field of AI but also the broader spectrum of science, technology, and human health.

8.2 The Road to Artificial General Intelligence (AGI)

Artificial General Intelligence (AGI), often referred to as "strong AI," represents the next monumental leap in the field of Artificial Intelligence. Unlike narrow or weak AI, which excels in specific tasks, AGI embodies the ability to understand, learn, and apply intelligence across a wide range of cognitive tasks at a human-like level. This section delves into the journey towards AGI, its potential implications, and the challenges along this ambitious path.

Understanding AGI

Definition and Distinction: AGI is defined as an AI system with the ability to comprehend, learn, and apply its intelligence to a broad spectrum of problems, akin to the cognitive capabilities of a human. This is in contrast to narrow AI, which is designed for specific tasks.

Characteristics of AGI: Key characteristics of AGI include adaptability, problem-solving skills in varied contexts, and the ability to process complex information and make autonomous decisions.

Progress and Current Research

Developments in AI: While considerable advancements have been made in narrow AI, the development of AGI remains in its nascent stages. Research in this area is focused on creating more flexible, adaptable AI systems that can generalize learning and apply it to a broader range of problems.

Interdisciplinary Approach: The pursuit of AGI is not only a technological challenge but also intersects with cognitive science, neuroscience, and philosophy, as it involves understanding and emulating complex aspects of human intelligence.

Challenges on the Road to AGI

Computational Complexity: Developing AGI involves immense computational challenges, requiring advanced algorithms that can mimic the diverse and dynamic nature of human thought processes.

Ethical and Safety Concerns: The creation of AGI raises significant ethical questions and safety concerns. It necessitates rigorous oversight to prevent unintended consequences and ensure that AGI systems align with human values and ethics.

Potential Implications of Achieving AGI

Transformational Impact: The realization of AGI could have a transformative impact on society, potentially solving complex global challenges, advancing scientific research, and reshaping various industries.

Economic and Social Changes: AGI could lead to significant changes in the job market, economy, and societal structures, requiring careful consideration and preparation for these shifts.

Summary

The road to Artificial General Intelligence is a journey filled with complex challenges, both technical and ethical. While advancements in narrow AI continue to progress rapidly, AGI remains a goal yet to be achieved, requiring breakthroughs in computational techniques and a deeper understanding of human cognition. The pursuit of AGI holds the promise of profound changes in our world, offering solutions to some of humanity's most pressing problems but also bringing forth significant societal and ethical considerations. As research and development in this area continue, the dream of creating machines with human-like intelligence and adaptability draws closer, potentially heralding a new era in AI and human history.

8.3 Predictions and Speculations about AI's Future

The future trajectory of Artificial Intelligence (AI) is a subject of great interest and speculation among technologists, business leaders, and academics. As AI continues to advance at a rapid pace, it prompts predictions and speculations about how it will shape our future. This section explores various forecasts and conjectures regarding the evolution of AI and its potential impact on society, technology, and global dynamics.

Technological Advancements

AI and Enhanced Cognitive Capabilities: Future AI systems are expected to exhibit more advanced cognitive capabilities, potentially surpassing human performance in various tasks.

Integration with Other Technologies: AI is likely to become more intertwined with other emerging technologies like the Internet of Things (IoT), blockchain, and augmented reality, leading to more integrated and intelligent systems.

Societal and Ethical Implications

Impact on Employment and the Economy: One of the most discussed topics is the impact of AI on jobs. While AI may automate certain roles, it is also expected to create new jobs and industries, albeit requiring different skill sets.

Ethical and Privacy Concerns: As AI becomes more pervasive, issues related to privacy, surveillance, and ethical use of AI will gain prominence. The need for robust ethical frameworks and regulations to guide AI development is anticipated to be a critical focus.

AI in Daily Life and Industry

AI in Everyday Life: Predictions suggest a future where AI is seamlessly integrated into daily life, from smart homes and personalized healthcare to autonomous transportation.

Industry Transformation: Industries such as healthcare, finance, education, and manufacturing are expected to undergo significant transformation due to AI, with increased efficiency, innovation, and new service offerings.

Global Dynamics

AI in Geopolitics: AI is set to play a crucial role in global dynamics, with nations investing heavily in AI for economic, military, and strategic advantages. AI's role in cybersecurity, warfare, and international relations is a topic of increasing relevance.

Digital Divide and Global Inequities: There is a concern that advancements in AI could exacerbate the digital divide and global inequities, with AI-rich countries gaining disproportionate advantages.

Long-Term Speculations

Artificial General Intelligence (AGI): The potential development of AGI, with cognitive abilities comparable to human intelligence, remains a speculative but transformative prospect.

Transhumanism and AI: Speculations about AI leading to transhumanism, where AI augments human capabilities and experiences, are prevalent in long-term forecasts.

Summary

Predictions and speculations about the future of AI encompass a wide range of possibilities, from technological advancements and societal transformations to ethical challenges and global dynamics. While there is excitement about AI's potential to revolutionize various aspects of life and work, there is also caution about its implications for employment, privacy, and societal equity. The future of AI is not just a technological narrative but a complex tapestry woven with economic, ethical, and geopolitical threads, indicating a future where AI will be integral to every facet of human existence.

CHAPTER 9

Getting Started with AI

Getting Started with AI provides a comprehensive guide for individuals interested in entering the field of Artificial Intelligence (AI). This section is designed to navigate the educational and career pathways in AI and highlight valuable resources and communities for AI enthusiasts.

Educational Pathways in AI (9.1)

This subsection outlines the various educational routes available for those seeking to delve into AI. It discusses formal education options like undergraduate and graduate degrees in computer science, AI, and related fields. It also highlights alternative learning paths, including online courses, boot camps, and self-learning resources. The importance of a strong foundation in mathematics, programming, and data science is emphasized for aspiring AI professionals.

Building a Career in AI: Skills and Roles (9.2)

Here, the focus is on the practical aspects of building a career in AI. The section details the essential skills required in the AI industry, such as machine learning, neural networks, natural language processing, and problem-solving abilities. It also explores various career roles within AI, including data scientists, machine learning engineers, AI researchers, and application developers. The discussion extends to the importance of soft skills and the need for continuous learning and adaptation in this rapidly evolving field.

Resources and Communities for AI Enthusiasts (9.3)

Recognizing the importance of community and ongoing learning in AI, this subsection provides a guide to various resources and communities. It lists popular online forums, AI research journals, conferences, and meetups where enthusiasts can stay updated with the latest AI trends, research, and networking opportunities. The section underscores the value of being part of a community for knowledge exchange, mentorship, and staying abreast of industry developments.

Section 9.0 serves as a practical roadmap for anyone interested in entering the field of AI. From educational foundations and career opportunities to engaging with the broader AI community, this section provides the essential tools and knowledge to start and progress in the dynamic and exciting world of AI.

9.1 Educational Pathways in AI

Artificial Intelligence (AI) is a rapidly evolving field, and the demand for skilled AI professionals is growing. Understanding the educational pathways to enter and excel in this field is vital. This section outlines the various educational options available, including leading universities offering specialized AI programs, online courses, and more.

Formal Education at Leading Universities

- **Undergraduate Programs**: Many top universities offer undergraduate degrees in computer science or related fields with a focus or specialization in AI. Examples include:
    - Massachusetts Institute of Technology (MIT)
    - Stanford University
    - Carnegie Mellon University
    - University of California, Berkeley
    - Harvard University
- **Graduate Programs**: For more specialized and advanced AI education, graduate programs are available. Prominent universities offering Master's and Ph.D. programs in AI, machine learning, and robotics include:
    - Stanford University
    - Carnegie Mellon University
    - Massachusetts Institute of Technology (MIT)
    - University of Cambridge
    - University of Oxford

Online Courses and Certifications

- **MOOCs**: Platforms like Coursera and edX collaborate with top universities to offer online courses in AI. These courses cater to various levels and include institutions like Stanford University and MIT.

- **Professional Certifications**: Companies like Google and IBM offer AI Professional Certificates, providing practical and industry-recognized qualifications.

Bootcamps and Workshops

- **AI Bootcamps**: These short, intensive programs are focused on practical AI skills. They are offered by various independent tech education providers.
- **Workshops and Seminars**: Regularly held by universities and tech companies, these events cover the latest AI trends and provide networking opportunities.

Self-Learning Resources

- **Online Tutorials and Forums**: Platforms such as Kaggle, GitHub, and Stack Overflow offer resources for self-directed learning in AI.
- **Books and Academic Journals**: A wide range of books, from introductory to advanced, cover AI topics. Academic journals provide insights into the latest research.

Extracurricular Activities

- **Hackathons and Competitions**: Participating in AI-related events can enhance practical skills.
- **Internships**: Internships in AI-focused companies or research labs offer valuable industry experience.

Summary

Educational pathways in AI are diverse and can accommodate different learning styles and career goals. Leading universities globally offer formal education programs in AI. Additionally, online courses, professional certifications, bootcamps, and self-study resources are widely available for those seeking alternative or supplementary learning methods. Practical experience, gained through internships and participation in AI projects and communities, is also crucial in developing a robust understanding and skill set in AI.

9.2 Building a Career in AI: Skills and Roles

Building a career in Artificial Intelligence (AI) offers a range of opportunities in one of the fastest-growing technology fields. The demand for skilled professionals is on the rise, making it a lucrative career choice. This section provides an overview of the necessary skills, various career roles, and an insight into the potential salary ranges in the AI industry.

Essential Skills for AI Careers

- **Programming Languages**: Proficiency in languages like Python, R, and Java is essential. Python is particularly popular due to its extensive AI and machine learning libraries.
- **Machine Learning and Algorithms**: Understanding various machine learning models and algorithms is crucial.
- **Data Analytics and Management**: The ability to process and analyze large datasets is key in AI.
- **Mathematical Skills**: Mathematics, especially linear algebra, calculus, and statistics, is foundational for AI.
- **Problem-Solving and Critical Thinking**: AI professionals must excel in solving complex problems and thinking critically.
- **Soft Skills**: Effective communication, teamwork, and ethical considerations are also important.

Career Roles and Salary Ranges in AI

- **Data Scientist**: Analyzes and interprets complex data. Average salary: $85,000 - $170,000 per year.
- **Machine Learning Engineer**: Creates AI models and systems. Average salary: $100,000 - $180,000 per year.
- **AI Research Scientist**: Conducts research to advance AI technology. Average salary: $110,000 - $220,000 per year.
- **AI Software Developer/Engineer**: Develops AI software solutions. Average salary: $90,000 - $160,000 per year.

- **Robotics Engineer**: Develops and programs robots. Average salary: $80,000 - $140,000 per year.
- **Business Intelligence Developer**: Uses AI for business analytics. Average salary: $75,000 - $130,000 per year.
- **AI Ethics Officer**: Ensures ethical AI development. Salary can vary widely depending on the industry and company size.

Emerging Roles

- **AI Policy Maker**: Works on AI regulations and policies. Salaries can vary based on the sector and location.
- **AI Product Manager**: Manages AI product development. Average salary: $90,000 - $150,000 per year.

Summary

A career in AI is not only intellectually challenging and rewarding but also offers lucrative financial benefits. While salary ranges vary depending on the specific role, location, and individual's experience, AI professionals are generally well-compensated. Essential technical skills, coupled with problem-solving abilities and soft skills, are key to success in this field. As AI continues to evolve, new roles are emerging, presenting more opportunities for those interested in this dynamic and exciting area of technology.

9.3 Resources and Communities for AI Enthusiasts

For individuals keen on exploring or advancing their knowledge in Artificial Intelligence (AI), a wealth of resources and communities are available. These platforms offer opportunities for learning, collaboration, and staying updated with the latest trends and developments in AI. This section provides a detailed overview of various resources and communities beneficial for AI enthusiasts at all levels.

Online Learning Platforms

- **Coursera, edX, and Udacity**: Offer a range of AI courses and specializations from top universities and institutions.
- **Kaggle**: Provides a platform for data science and machine learning competitions, datasets, and a community forum for discussions and collaboration.
- **ai**: Offers practical and free courses focused on deep learning and machine learning.

Professional Associations and Organizations

- **Association for the Advancement of Artificial Intelligence (AAAI)**: A prestigious organization for AI professionals, offering conferences, publications, and resources.
- **IEEE Computational Intelligence Society**: Provides resources, professional development, and networking opportunities in AI and computational intelligence.
- **OpenAI**: An AI research lab that shares research papers, tools, and resources with the aim of promoting and developing friendly AI.

Communities and Forums

- **Reddit (subreddits like r/MachineLearning, r/artificial, r/deeplearning)**: Active online communities discussing AI topics, research, and news.
- **Stack Overflow**: A valuable resource for coding and technical questions related to AI and machine learning.
- **GitHub**: Hosts a multitude of AI projects and code repositories, facilitating collaboration and sharing of AI software and tools.

Conferences and Meetups

- **NeurIPS, ICML, CVPR**: Leading international conferences in AI, offering insights into cutting-edge research and networking opportunities.
- **Local Meetup Groups**: Many cities have local meetup groups for AI enthusiasts, offering seminars, workshops, and networking events.

Books and Journals

- **Books**: Titles like "Artificial Intelligence: A Modern Approach" by Stuart Russell and Peter Norvig, and "Deep Learning" by Ian Goodfellow, Yoshua Bengio, and Aaron Courville, are highly recommended.
- **Journals**: Publications like the Journal of Artificial Intelligence Research (JAIR) and Artificial Intelligence provide scholarly articles and research findings.

Podcasts and Blogs

- **Podcasts**: Shows like "AI in Business" and "The AI Podcast" offer insights from industry experts.
- **Blogs**: AI-focused blogs by companies like OpenAI, Google AI Blog, and individuals in the AI field are great for keeping up with news and developments.

Summary

For AI enthusiasts, the resources and communities available are vast and varied. From online courses and professional organizations to active online forums and prestigious conferences, these platforms provide invaluable learning and networking opportunities. Engaging with these resources can enhance knowledge, foster community interactions, and keep one abreast of the latest advancements in the field of AI. Whether one is a beginner or an experienced professional, these resources serve as vital tools for growth and engagement in the dynamic and ever-evolving world of AI.

CHAPTER 10

Summary

Thank you so much for reading this book. I hope it has given you a good start with programming in Assembly language.

The sample programs in this book are structured to provide you with each of these features in a step-by-step manner so that you can learn each of these concepts in a short amount of time. The best way to learn to program is to learn a little bit at a time and to continue to practice for an extended period, so you improve day by day. In the introduction of this book, I provide a link to the online version of this class that you can sign up for, which contains videos and additional information. You can also download the code for any of the programs in this book from that class.

If you have suggestions for improving this book, I would love to hear from you. Please leave a review and or contact me at sales@destinlearning.com. You can also sign up for my newsletter at http://destinlearning.com where I publish updates about the new material that I have produced.

Thank you again.

10.1 About the Author

I have worked in software development and IT operations for 30 years as a Software Developer, Software Development Manager, Software Architect and Operations Manager. For the last ten years, I have taught evening courses on various IT related subjects at several local universities in the central Ohio area. In 2015 I founded http://destinlearning.com, and have developed a series of online courses and books that can provide practical information to students on various IT and software development topics.

If you would like to connect with me on social medial you can connect with me on LinkedIn at the following address:

https://www.linkedin.com/in/efrick/

14.2 More From Destin Learning

Thank you so much for your interest in this book. I hope it has given you a good start in the exciting field of database management. If you would like to learn more about information technology, you can check out my book, Information Technology Essentials.

Information Technology Essentials

You can see this course and more on my website:

https://www.destinlearning.com

10.3 Destin Learning YouTube Channel

You can see more on my YouTube channel, where I am continuing to post free videos about software development and information technology and career development. If you subscribe to my channel, you will get updates as I post new material weekly.

https://youtube.com/destinlearning

Appendix A: Glossary of AI Term

Algorithm: A set of rules or instructions given to an AI program to help it learn and make decisions.

Artificial Intelligence (AI): The simulation of human intelligence processes by machines, especially computer systems. These processes include learning, reasoning, self-correction, and more.

Artificial Neural Network (ANN): Computational models inspired by the human brain, consisting of interconnected nodes that process information in a way similar to the way neurons operate in the brain.

Backpropagation: An algorithm used in training neural networks, where the model adjusts its parameters (weights) based on the error rate obtained in the previous epoch (iteration).

Big Data: Extremely large data sets that may be analyzed computationally to reveal patterns, trends, and associations.

Classification: A machine learning approach where a model is trained to categorize input data into various classes.

Clustering: A type of unsupervised learning where an AI algorithm groups data points into distinct sub-groups or clusters based on similarities.

Convolutional Neural Network (CNN): A type of deep neural network often used to analyze visual imagery, structured in layers to recognize features and patterns.

Data Mining: The practice of examining large pre-existing databases to generate new information and insights.

Deep Learning: A subset of machine learning in artificial intelligence that has networks capable of learning unsupervised from data that is unstructured or unlabeled.

Expert System: An AI system that emulates the decision-making ability of a human expert, typically in a specific domain.

Feature Extraction: The process of reducing the number of resources required to describe large sets of data accurately.

Heuristics: Techniques that help in problem-solving, learning, and discovery.

Machine Learning (ML): A subset of AI that provides systems the ability to automatically learn and improve from experience without being explicitly programmed.

Natural Language Processing (NLP): The ability of a computer program to understand, interpret, and generate human language.

Neural Network: See Artificial Neural Network (ANN).

Reinforcement Learning: A type of machine learning where an agent learns to behave in an environment by performing actions and seeing the results.

Supervised Learning: A type of machine learning where the model is trained on a labeled dataset.

TensorFlow: An open-source software library for dataflow and differentiable programming across a range of tasks, widely used for machine learning applications such as neural networks.

Unsupervised Learning: A type of machine learning where the model is trained on unlabeled data without any guidance.

Weights: The parameters within a neural network that transform input data within the network's hidden layers.

This glossary provides a foundational understanding of key terms and concepts in the field of AI, beneficial for navigating the more complex discussions and applications of AI technology.

Appendix B Quiz 2.4
Answers

Who proposed the Turing Test, a benchmark for determining a machine's capability to exhibit intelligent behavior? a) Alan Turing b) John McCarthy c) Marvin Minsky d) Isaac Newton
Correct Answer: a) Alan Turing

At which event was the term "Artificial Intelligence" first coined? a) The Dartmouth Conference (1956) b) The Turing Conference (1950) c) The MIT AI Conference (1960) d) The Stanford Symposium (1955)
Correct Answer: a) The Dartmouth Conference (1956)

Which of the following is considered an early form of AI in history? a) Calculators b) Mechanical Clocks c) Renaissance Automata d) Telegraph Machines
Correct Answer: c) Renaissance Automata

What was a significant achievement in AI during the 1990s? a) The creation of the World Wide Web b) The development of the first chatbot c) IBM's Deep Blue defeating chess champion Garry Kasparov d) The launch of the first smartphone
Correct Answer: c) IBM's Deep Blue defeating chess champion Garry Kasparov

What does Symbolic AI focus on? a) Neural networks b) Rule-based systems and logical reasoning c) Data mining d) Quantum computing
Correct Answer: b) Rule-based systems and logical reasoning

Who developed the concept of Boolean Logic, which is foundational in AI? a) Alan Turing b) John von Neumann c) George Boole d) Ada Lovelace
Correct Answer: c) George Boole

What marked the beginning of the 'AI Winter' in the 1980s? a) Lack of interest in AI b) Reduction in AI research funding c) Overhyped AI expectations d) Technical

limitations in computing power
Correct Answer: b) Reduction in AI research funding

Which development signified a major shift in AI from rule-based systems to learning algorithms? a) The introduction of expert systems b) The rise of machine learning c) The development of the first neural network d) The invention of the microprocessor
Correct Answer: b) The rise of machine learning

What is the primary focus of 'Deep Learning' within AI? a) Data privacy b) Logical reasoning c) Neural networks with many layers d) Symbolic language processing
Correct Answer: c) Neural networks with many layers

Which of the following was an early expert system used in AI? a) ELIZA b) DENDRAL c) Watson d) Siri
Correct Answer: b) DENDRAL

Appendix C Quiz 3.4
Answers

Q1 Which of the following best describes artificial intelligence (AI)?

1. The ability of a computer to perform tasks that normally require human intelligence
2. The process of improving computer hardware
3. The study of biological neural networks
4. The use of mathematics to solve complex problems **Answer:** a) The ability of a computer to perform tasks that normally require human intelligence

Q2: What is a key difference between human intelligence and artificial intelligence?

1. AI can process information faster than human intelligence
2. Humans use electricity to think, while AI does not
3. AI is capable of emotional reasoning
4. Humans require data to learn, while AI does not **Answer:** a) AI can process information faster than human intelligence

Q3: What is an algorithm in the context of artificial intelligence?

1. A device used for computing
2. A set of rules or instructions designed to solve a problem
3. A type of computer hardware
4. A database system **Answer:** b) A set of rules or instructions designed to solve a problem

Q:4 Why is data important in artificial intelligence?

1. It provides a source of energy for AI systems
2. It is used to train and improve AI algorithms
3. Data is not important in AI
4. It is used to make AI systems look more realistic **Answer:** b) It is used to train and improve AI algorithms

Q5: What is machine learning in the context of AI?

1. A process where machines develop their own hardware
2. The ability of AI systems to learn from and make decisions based on data
3. A marketing term for advanced AI
4. The study of mechanical engineering **Answer:** b) The ability of AI systems to learn from and make decisions based on data

Q6: Which of the following is NOT a type of machine learning?

1. Supervised learning
2. Unsupervised learning
3. Transductive learning
4. Reactive learning **Answer:** d) Reactive learning

Q7: What distinguishes deep learning from traditional machine learning?

1. Deep learning is exclusively based on linear algorithms
2. Deep learning involves neural networks with many layers
3. Deep learning does not use algorithms
4. Deep learning is another term for supervised learning **Answer:** b) Deep learning involves neural networks with many layers

Q8: What is a neural network in the context of AI?

1. A network of computers connected to each other
2. A system that mimics the human brain to process information
3. A type of database used in AI systems
4. A tool for repairing physical neural connections in the brain **Answer:** b) A system that mimics the human brain to process information

Q9: Which of the following is an application of artificial intelligence?

1. Manual record-keeping
2. Natural language processing
3. Traditional book printing
4. Non-digital art creation **Answer:** b) Natural language processing

Q10: How has AI evolved over time?

1. AI has remained largely the same since its inception
2. AI has evolved from simple rule-based systems to complex learning systems
3. AI has decreased in capability due to hardware limitations
4. AI has shifted focus from data processing to mechanical tasks **Answer:** b) AI has evolved from simple rule-based systems to complex learning systems

Appendix D Quiz 4.6
Answers

Which branch of AI focuses on teaching computers to learn from and improve upon past experiences? a) Computer Vision b) Robotics c) Machine Learning d) Natural Language Processing
Correct Answer: c) Machine Learning

Natural Language Processing (NLP) is primarily concerned with: a) Interpreting and generating human language b) Recognizing and analyzing visual data c) Building and programming robots d) Creating rule-based systems for decision-making
Correct Answer: a) Interpreting and generating human language

Robotics in AI is mainly about: a) Developing algorithms for machine learning b) Machines that can see and interpret the world c) Creating machines that can perform tasks autonomously d) Analyzing large datasets
Correct Answer: c) Creating machines that can perform tasks autonomously

What is the main focus of Computer Vision in AI? a) Enhancing human-computer interaction b) Enabling machines to visually interpret the world c) Automating manufacturing processes d) Translating different languages
Correct Answer: b) Enabling machines to visually interpret the world

Expert Systems in AI are designed to: a) Emulate human physical abilities b) Mimic human decision-making expertise c) Understand and generate natural language d) Recognize and interpret images and videos
Correct Answer: b) Mimic human decision-making expertise

Which type of learning involves AI systems being trained on labeled data? a) Unsupervised Learning b) Supervised Learning c) Reinforcement Learning d) Deep Learning
Correct Answer: b) Supervised Learning

In NLP, what technique is used to determine the sentiment or emotional tone behind text? a) Object Recognition b) Sentiment Analysis c) Image Classification d) Reinforcement Learning
Correct Answer: b) Sentiment Analysis

Which AI field involves designing intelligent agents that interact with their environment? a) Machine Learning b) Robotics c) Computer Vision d) Expert Systems
Correct Answer: b) Robotics

Deep Learning, a subset of Machine Learning, is primarily based on: a) Logical rules and algorithms b) Neural networks with multiple layers c) Language processing algorithms d) Robotic control systems
Correct Answer: b) Neural networks with multiple layers

What is a key application of Computer Vision? a) Automated translation of languages b) Predicting stock market trends c) Facial recognition and image analysis d) Rule-based problem-solving
Correct Answer: c) Facial recognition and image analysis

Appendix E Quiz 6.4
Answers

Q1: What is a primary ethical consideration in AI development?

1. Maximizing profit margins
2. Ensuring AI systems are entertaining
3. Making AI systems as complex as possible
4. Ensuring AI systems do not cause harm

Answer: d) Ensuring AI systems do not cause harm

Q2: Why is it important to consider the societal impact of AI?

1. It is important only for marketing purposes
2. AI can have significant effects on employment, privacy, and fairness
3. Society has little influence on AI development
4. AI development does not impact society

Answer: b) AI can have significant effects on employment, privacy, and fairness

Q3: What causes bias in AI systems?

1. Bias in AI systems is always intentional
2. Biased data used in training the AI
3. AI systems are inherently unbiased
4. Bias is only caused by hardware malfunctions

Answer: b) Biased data used in training the AI

Q4: How can fairness be promoted in AI systems?

1. By ignoring the data
2. By using only one type of algorithm
3. By ensuring diverse and representative data
4. Fairness is not a concern in AI

Answer: c) By ensuring diverse and representative data

Q5: Why is privacy a concern in AI?

1. AI systems do not affect privacy
2. AI can process and store large amounts of personal data
3. Privacy concerns are only relevant for social media
4. AI systems are incapable of accessing private data

Answer: b) AI can process and store large amounts of personal data

Q6: What is a security risk associated with AI?

1. AI systems cannot be hacked
2. AI always improves security
3. Vulnerability to cyber attacks and data breaches
4. AI systems are too simple to pose security risks

Answer: c) Vulnerability to cyber attacks and data breaches

Q7: Who should be held accountable for decisions made by AI systems?

1. Only the AI system itself
2. The developers and organizations behind the AI systems
3. AI systems do not make decisions
4. Accountability is not applicable to AI

Answer: b) The developers and organizations behind the AI systems

Q8: Why is transparency important in AI systems?

1. It is only important for aesthetic reasons
2. Transparency helps build trust and allows for better understanding of AI decisions
3. AI systems are naturally transparent
4. Transparency has no impact on AI

Answer: b) Transparency helps build trust and allows for better understanding of AI decisions

Q9: How can AI impact human rights?

1. AI has no impact on human rights
2. By potentially affecting privacy, freedom of expression, and non-discrimination
3. Human rights are a concern only for manual processes
4. AI improves human rights by default

Answer: b) By potentially affecting privacy, freedom of expression, and non-discrimination

Q10: What is a method to mitigate bias in AI systems?

1. Using the same data for every AI system
2. Ignoring user feedback
3. Regularly reviewing and updating datasets and algorithms
4. Bias cannot be mitigated in AI systems

Answer: c) Regularly reviewing and updating datasets and algorithms

Appendix F Access to Online Course

By purchasing this book, you will also receive free access to the video version of this class on my website. You can access this class by using the following link:

https://www.destinlearning.com/courses/introduction-to-artificial-intelligence?coupon=AI2024

If you have any difficulties signing up, please contact me at sales@destinlearning.com and I will send you a coupon code. Thank you again for purchasing this book. If you have any feedback, please contact me. I want to make this book and course the very best they can be.